Best Practice in the Early Years

Alistair Bryce-Clegg

BLOOMSBURY
LONDON · OXFORD · NEW YORK · NEW DELHI · SYDNEY

Bloomsbury Education

An imprint of Bloomsbury Publishing Plc

50 Bedford Square	1385 Broadway
London	New York
WC1B 3DP	NY 10018
UK	USA

www.bloomsbury.com

BLOOMSBURY and the Diana logo are trademarks of Bloomsbury Publishing Plc

First published in 2015

ISBN: PB: 9781441138347
ePub: 9781441177353
ePDF: 9781441149480

6 8 10 9 7

Typeset by Newgen Knowledge Works (P) Ltd., Chennai, India
Printed and bound in Great Britain by CPI Group (UK) Ltd, Croydon CR0 4YY

This book is produced using paper that is made from wood grown in managed, sustainable forests. It is natural, renewable and recyclable. The logging and manufacturing processes conform to the environmental regulations of the country of origin.

To find out more about our authors and books visit www.bloomsbury.com. Here you will find extracts, author interviews, details of forthcoming events and the option to sign up for our newsletters.

With thanks to Sally Featherstone for her consultancy work on this book and to the staff and children at LEYF for their help with the photographs.

The Blackpool Transition Project (page 130) is reproduced by kind permission of Blackpool Council.

Contents

Introduction

So, you want to know more about best practice in the Early Years as you aspire to be the best practitioner that you can be? Well, I suppose you must, otherwise you wouldn't have bought (or borrowed) this book!

The fact that you are interested enough in your own practice to pick up this book in the first place is a good start, as one of the key ingredients of best practice is to be a reflective practitioner. No matter how long you have been doing it, no matter how much of a success or disaster your session or your day was, it is always good to reflect on what you are doing.

As well as days where we feel we have excelled (never the day that anyone comes to watch us teach!), we also all have days that we think we have failed miserably (usually the day when someone comes to watch us teach). It is important that we recognise both these states of being, and spend as much time reflecting on why something went well as we do on why it went badly.

Although there is an entertainer in every good practitioner, best Early Years practice has far more to do with the quality of the environment, the planning and the teaching than it does on the teacher standing out. This is why Ofsted, and I hope your managers too, will in future be looking at the contribution you are making to best practice in your setting, not just whether you are that single magical outstanding teacher/practitioner.

During a recent observation of a Reception teacher alongside their headteacher, the head said 'Can I ask you a question? Do all Early Years teachers sound like candidates for the asthma clinic?' At first I didn't get what he was saying, but once the teacher got into full swing all became apparent. Every sentence was punctuated with a loud gasp or intake of breath, primarily done, I think, to engender an air of excitement around proceedings, but very quickly losing impact. Apart, that is, from on one poor boy who had created a model of sheer magnificence out of plastic construction bricks. He came up behind his beloved teacher to show her the thing of beauty that he had produced. Seeing him out of the corner of her eye, she both swung round and gasped at the same time. This action did not solicit a response of joy from the boy, but instead one of shock. Rather than hold forth his model and experience a moment of pride, the noise of the sudden gasp caused an adrenalin surge and his arms involuntarily flung the model high into the air. We all stood and watched as, almost in slow motion, his three story superhero hideaway went crashing to the ground and resumed its former existence as a pile of construction bricks! So, a little gasping can be a good thing in attracting attention to something you want to be noticed – but don't overdo it!

There are many complex elements of best practice which practitioners hone over time with knowledge and experience. So, by reading this book, I cannot promise to 'make' you into that outstanding contributor to outstanding provision. What I can do, however, is share some ideas around 'best' Early Years practice that have had a significant positive impact on the wellbeing, progress and attainment of children from pre-school to Year One in a wide variety of settings. These ideas, mixed with your own drive for improvement and a lot of self-reflection, will get you well on the way to being confident in your own practice and in turn you will be able to explain how it enables children to be effective learners.

It's easy to provide a cabaret act in front of children who are captivated by the performance, but remember nothing once it ends. Effective practice is almost invisible, and the change it makes is only evident when you look at the children, and observe how they have changed. Of course this doesn't mean that being an effective practitioner is easy – it isn't! It takes a lot of work, a lot of preparation and a lot of self-control, as you plan for activity, prepare your environment, and then stand back as the children interact with the environment you have created.

Sometimes it can be frustrating when the people who are making judgements about your practice don't quite see things in the same way as you do. As well as helping you to become a more effective practitioner, this book will help you to articulate why your practice is the way that it is, and enable you to hone it to a point where *you* can recognise high-level elements of it, long before you try to convince anyone else!

In the chapters of this book, I have focused on the following aspects of effective teaching and learning:

- Using the Characteristics of Effective Learning to help you to focus on providing a high quality environment where children can become active thinkers;
- How you can underpin learning by supporting and evaluating children's sense of wellbeing and engagement in their learning;
- The place of formative and summative assessment in tracking progress and locating attainment;
- Constructing and analysing progress *and* attainment through GSA (Gap and Strength Analysis);
- Organising and planning for basic and continuous provision;
- Making sense of skill development by unpacking pure and facilitative skills;
- Direct teaching and how this can take many forms, from whole-class teaching to objective-led teaching;
- Making sure that display reflects children's learning, not just the artistic talents of the adults;
- The effective use of role play to enhance children's interests;
- Effective ways to inspire children;
- How to organise your day effectively;
- Making sure that children make a smooth and positive transition from your setting or class to the next stage of their learning.

1 An environment for effective learning

'Children are highly motivated, very eager to join in and consistently demonstrate the characteristics of effective learning with high levels of curiosity, imagination and concentration.'

(Grade descriptors of Outstanding Progress – effectiveness of the early years provision;
The School Inspection Handbook; Ofsted; 2014)

In this chapter, I will explore the Characteristics of Effective Learning from the Framework for the Early Years Foundation Stage (EYFS), and unpack these in some detail, with a simple series of questions, which you can use in your own settings. An effective environment for learning is *active*, a frequently used description, which I explore next, following this with some information on the importance of thinking skills in the Early Years, and looking at the concept of an environment for thinking. Before our quest for 'effective practice' begins in earnest it makes great sense to start with what we know about how children learn effectively and acknowledge how we need to translate this information into our environments and everyday teaching.

The Characteristics of Effective Learning

The main (inspection) evidence comes from inspectors' direct observations of the way in which children demonstrate the key Characteristics of Effective Learning:

- *playing and exploring*
- *active learning*
- *creating and thinking critically*

and their evaluation of how practitioners' teaching facilitates children's learning.
(*Evaluation schedule for inspections of registered early years provision; Ofsted; 2014*)

The Characteristics of Effective Learning should underpin everything that we do in our EYFS environments. They are rooted in the science of how children learn, and therefore should guide and support the ways in which we create learning spaces, and how we teach.

Although I am sure that you are all very familiar with them, it is worth reminding ourselves of their importance before we go on.

Like sacred amulets, there are three of them. Each powerful in their own right, but together their combined power is immense! In unpacking these, I have posed some simple questions which you might ask as you examine your own practice.

Characteristics of Effective Learning
Playing and exploring – engagement   Finding out and exploring   Playing with what they know   Being willing to 'have a go'
Active learning – motivation   Being involved and concentrating   Keeping trying   Enjoying achieving what they set out to do
Creating and thinking critically – thinking   Having their own ideas   Making links   Choosing ways to do things

(The Characteristics of Effective Learning; Statutory Framework for the Early Years Foundation Stage; DfE; 2012)

So how should we bring these simple criteria to life in our own settings and classrooms, and what will inspectors and others who observe our practice be looking for? Much of what is implied will be familiar to experienced practitioners working in the EYFS, but the emphasis has clearly been sharpened to focus on *how* children learn, not simply *what* they learn, and has moved the spotlight onto *progress*, rather than simply looking at *attainment*.

Some definitions:

__Progress__: this is the extent to which pupils have progressed in their learning from their starting points and capabilities

__Attainment__: this is the standard of academic attainment, typically shown by test and examination results

__Achievement__: this takes into account the standards of attainment reached by pupils and the progress they have made to reach those standards

(Inspection Guidance; DfE/Ofsted; 2012)

Without doubt, from 2015, inspectors and others will be looking even more closely at how much progress children are making, whether they are in an adult-led activity or in activities that they initiate themselves:

> For those schools where children are aged three and four years and move to primary school before any nationally comparable assessments are made, the judgement should be based on an evaluation of children's learning and progress relative to their age and evidence of their starting points.

> (The School Inspection Handbook; Ofsted; January 2015)

In this chapter I will be looking at the way that each of the Characteristics of Effective Learning has been expanded into a series of statements within the Guidance for the EYFS, and how each of these statements raises questions for us, when thinking about provision in our settings. Let's look at some of the questions you could ask yourselves.

Playing and exploring

How do you know if you are fostering an environment that actively encourages children to play and explore? What exactly do we mean by 'play and explore' anyway?

In some circles these days 'play' has almost become a 'four letter word'! The problem is that some people don't make the essential connection between play and learning. We need to make sure that we understand how the environment that we create not only allows children to have lots of opportunities to play freely, but also supports their learning through implicit and explicit challenge.

When we talk about 'exploring' we don't just mean putting on your backpack and heading off into the woods (although it can mean that). What we need to ask is where are the opportunities for children to 'explore' in every area of your provision?

Take your small world area for example – where are the opportunities for exploration and investigation? Do you have open-ended resources that will encourage creative and critical thinking as well as imagination? Have you created an environment for true 'exploration'?

While all children need an initial concrete point of reference, a good learning environment has lots of elements of 'ambiguity' or 'open-endedness', resources that are open to interpretation and exploration depending on who is holding them in their hand.

Ask yourself the following questions about playing and exploring.

Finding out and exploring

- What areas and activities are your children drawn to, both as individuals and groups?
- Do they initiate activities themselves or always join an existing one?
- Can they think aloud and describe what they do?

Using what they know in their play

- Do children draw on their own experiences from home?
- Do children act out real life and fantasy situations as part of their role play?
- Are children confident in finding tools, materials and resources they need for a particular project?

Being willing to have a go

- Do children show persistence?
- Are children keen to try new ideas or do they tend to stick with the familiar?
- Are children able to talk about what they have done?
- Can children identify things that haven't worked and give possible reasons why?
- Do children need adult support or can they initiate their own play themselves?

Active learning

This element doesn't just refer to children's ability to be physically active, but rather their level of mental activity. Do children show engagement, concentration and resilience when they are attempting a task? Do children show a 'can do' attitude to the majority of aspects of their learning rather than an 'I can't' attitude?

How actively a child engages in their learning will depend a great deal on how interesting and relevant the learning opportunity is that has been presented to them.

To encourage children to be active learners, ensure that you create an environment led by their interests. Give them lots of different opportunities for learning on their own, with a partner, as part of a group and alongside an adult.

Ask yourself the following questions about active learning.

Being involved and concentrating

- Do children stay focused on a self-initiated activity for a long period of time?
- Do children show high levels of concentration without distraction?
- Do they show high levels of focus and interest in what they are doing?
- Do they demonstrate concentration through silent focused work or by talking out loud as they play?

Keeping on trying

- Do children show persistence, not giving up, even if it means starting again?
- Do they ask for help and support if they need it?
- Do they discuss solutions for challenges with their friends and adults in the setting or do they prefer to work it through for themselves?

Enjoying and achieving what they set out to do

- Is there a sense of satisfaction and pride when they have completed an activity?
- Do children relish a challenge, happy to revisit something to improve it and make it better?
- Do they evaluate their own achievements and do things differently as a result?
- Are they intrinsically motivated, achieving things for themselves as opposed to just looking for praise?

Creating and thinking critically

Creativity and critical thinking are processes that are child led but which benefit greatly from the sensitive contributions of others. The processes involve making connections between things, people or places in ways that are new and personally meaningful. They occur in all areas of Learning and Development. (EYFS; 2007)

This characteristic of learning is all about creative and critical thinking, and this sort of thinking is hard work! We need to give our children lots of opportunities to think, puzzle and work things out on their own and with others. At times in their development they will need a lot of scaffolding and support for their thinking, but at others they will need the opportunity to think for themselves – and that can be a little bit scary!

We are aware that babies and young children are thinkers who make sense of their experiences through perceiving patterns and developing concepts. As children engage in all the different activities, which take place in the Early Years setting, they begin to be more actively involved in think about the meaning of what they are doing. Over time they

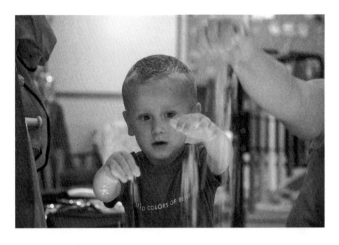

will begin to become more aware of their own thinking – called metacognition – thinking about thinking.

The more you focus on recognising different children's approaches to learning, the more skilled you will become at 'interpreting' what you see and then feeding that knowledge back into your environment and planning. The more you improve your own knowledge about how children learn then the more you will see when you watch them in play and learning.

Ask yourself the following questions about creating and thinking critically.

Having their own ideas

- Do the children try something different rather than just follow what someone else has done?
- Do they show both scaffolded and independent thinking strategies for addressing problems?
- Do they retain their independence, not asking for help even if it takes them longer to complete the task?

Using what they already know to learn new things

- Do they understand patterns and predict events?
- Can they talk about how what they are doing or how their thinking links to a previous event or experience?
- Do they draw upon knowledge or experience that is not immediately related to this activity?

Choosing ways to do things and finding new ways

- Are they confident in using trial and error approaches and talking about why some things do and some things don't work?
- Do they choose different ways of approaching activities and adapting that approach if it doesn't work?

An environment for thinking

The third Characteristic of Effective Learning, Creating and Thinking Critically, is certainly the most important for long-term success in education and in life – without thinking we become less than human, as Descartes said – 'I think therefore I am'. So thinking is a skill we learn as we grow, and children need plenty of practice in thinking about what they are learning, feeling and exploring.

Of course, there are levels of thinking – we sometimes think about the mundane and necessary, the day-to-day 'stuff' that keeps life running smoothly but when we have opportunities to take our thinking beyond the mundane, we open up the possibilities for real creativity and innovation. Children need these opportunities too, and often in their fast-paced lives there is little time to reflect and think deeply.

The opportunity to engage in creative and critical thinking excites, motivates and enhances learning and discovery for children and adults alike. A great learning environment is also a great thinking environment, where adults and children are developing and applying thinking strategies, accepting differences, hypothesising and extending their thinking by the use of ever expanding vocabularies.

As Early Years practitioners, we have the capacity to create environments, plan experiences and model strategies that give our children the tools and the opportunities to become truly great thinkers.

So what makes a good thinking environment – one where children can learn new thinking skills, but then be given the opportunity to apply them?

There are three primary strands to an effective thinking environment:

- The adults have a clear understanding of the characteristics of the children's learning and thinking, and how they can be identified and evaluated – this is not about *what* your children have learned, but *how* they learn, their particular motivations, personal preferences and learning styles.
- The role of the adult – it is the adults who will be responsible for creating the environment that supports children's learning styles and then facilitating opportunities for effective and productive thinking.

- The physical environment – an environment that will support children in clarifying what they already know while giving them opportunities to extend their thinking.

Before you can enhance children's thinking spaces, you need to first recognise how they think and learn.

An environment for effective active learning

An 'environment for effective active learning' sounds like such an obvious statement. What other sort of environment would we want to create for our children to learn in? It is only when we begin to unpick what 'effective learning' might look like that we begin to see the complexities of the task in hand.

Whatever the size and shape of your space, your environment has the potential to make a significant impact on children's levels of engagement. The key is to make sure that children feel ownership of the space and that how you have arranged the resources and the content of your display are for the children and not you.

When thinking about planning for your environment, it's important to remember that it encompasses both indoors and outside. Outdoor provision is such a crucial part of the EYFS curriculum that it should receive equal weighting in terms of planning and resourcing as indoors. Unfortunately, it is often the poor relation and the lack of provision results in a huge number of missed opportunities, especially for those children who can be harder to engage.

A good Early Years environment will always have a healthy amount of child-generated mess on any given day, such as the odd handprint on the wall, splash of paint on the lino or unidentifiable stain on the carpet! Notice that I say 'child-generated' mess – there is a significant difference between the mess that children make when they are engaged in a learning process and the sort of mess that adults leave lying around. We must remember that we are creating and maintaining a learning environment for children, and any adult 'stuff' should be filed or piled in a cupboard or drawer and not left on display for all to see.

I am a firm believer that a good EYFS environment should be fluid, and by that I mean that children should be able to take resources between areas and not be restricted to 'between these two sets of shelves is our mark-making area', and there will be significant punishments for any child who takes a mark maker anywhere else!

We must be more receptive to the fact that children don't learn in a predictable 'single area of learning' way, their learning ranges all over the place, and if Nathan has a lump of dough and wants to take it to the workshop and stick some 'fandango feathers' in it and then take it into the role-play area as his pet – then he should be able to do that. We are supposed to be creating environments that allow children to learn through play-based discovery and well-planned activities. You can't learn much if everything has to stay within its own three-foot square area. Young children will also be displaying perfectly normal developmental behaviours (often referred to as schemas) as they enjoy transporting objects – that is the nature of children's development and should be encouraged!

This chapter has examined how the environment for effective learning can be enhanced when we, as practitioners:

- look carefully at the implications of the EYFS guidance
- focus on how thinking skills will help children to learn.

2 Ensuring wellbeing

Criteria for outstanding support for children's wellbeing in Early Years settings have recently been published by Ofsted, and include these:

- *All practitioners are highly skilled and sensitive in helping children of all ages form secure emotional attachments, and provide a strong base for helping them in developing their independence and ability to explore.*
- *Children increasingly show high levels of self-control during activities and confidence in social situations, and are developing an excellent understanding of how to manage risks and challenges relative to their age.*
- *Children's safety and safeguarding is central to everything all practitioners do. They effectively support children's growing understanding of how to keep themselves safe and healthy.*
- *There is a highly stimulating environment with child-accessible resources that promote learning and challenge children both in and outdoors.*
- *The strong skills of all key persons ensure all children are emotionally well prepared for the next stages in their learning. Practitioners skillfully support children's transitions both within the setting and to other settings and school.*

(Guidance for Inspectors of Early Years settings; Ofsted; 2014)

It is heartening to see that Ofsted have noticed the omission of wellbeing from the inspection guidance, and have given their inspectors (and practitioners) some helpful advice on what to look for. In this chapter, I will explore how children's wellbeing can be monitored, using a well established tool, the Leuven Scales developed by Professor Ferre Leavers, and now a well established and welcome addition to effective assessment in the Early Years. I will also explore other aspects of effective learning which have not been given a high enough profile in the current guidance for practitioners and teachers working in the Foundation Stage.

Wellbeing – the missing element. How do we ensure and monitor children's sense of wellbeing?

More and more in the settings I work with, practitioners are encouraged to assess children's academic attainment above all else. The truth of the matter is that if children are not at ease within the learning environment and not engaged by what they are being asked to do (and how they are being asked to do it) they will not learn effectively. Children who feel positive, engaged and involved will learn better, and settings where children's sense of wellbeing is nurtured are the most effective in ensuring high quality outcomes.

One tool that can be used to help to create an effective learning environment and monitor its effectiveness, is the Leuven Scales of Well-being and Involvement.

The Leuven Scales were developed by the Research Centre for Experiential Education at Leuven University, under the supervision of Professor Ferre Laevers, and have become a well-recognised and welcome addition to effective assessment. Wellbeing refers to children's self-esteem, self-confidence and resilience, described by the Leuven institute as when children behave 'like fish in water'!

> *The tool focuses on two central indicators of quality early years provision: children's 'well-being' and 'involvement'. Well-being refers to feeling at ease, being spontaneous and free of emotional tensions and is crucial to good 'mental health'. Well-being is linked to self-confidence, a good degree of self-esteem and resilience. Involvement refers to being intensely engaged in activities and is considered to be a necessary condition for deep level learning and development.*
>
> (Observing Learning, Playing and Interacting in the EYFS; Plymouth City Council; 2011)

The tool focuses on two indicators of quality Early Years (wellbeing and involvement), and describes five levels within each scale.

The Wellbeing scale focuses on the extent to which pupils feel at ease, act spontaneously, show vitality and self-confidence. It is a crucial component of emotional intelligence and good mental health.

Level	Wellbeing	Signals
1.	Extremely low	The child clearly shows signs of discomfort such as crying or screaming. They may look dejected, sad, frightened or angry. The child does not respond to the environment, avoids contact and is withdrawn. The child may behave aggressively, hurting him/herself or others.
2.	Low	The posture, facial expression and actions indicate that the child does not feel at ease. However, the signals are less explicit than under level 1 or the sense of discomfort is not expressed the whole time.
3.	Moderate	The child has a neutral posture. Facial expression and posture show little or no emotion. There are no signs indicating sadness or pleasure, comfort or discomfort.
4.	High	The child shows obvious signs of satisfaction (as listed under level 5). However, these signals are not constantly present with the same intensity.
5.	Extremely high	The child looks happy and cheerful, smiles, cries out with pleasure. They may be lively and full of energy. Actions can be spontaneous and expressive. The child may talk to him/herself, play with sounds, hum, sing. The child appears relaxed and does not show any signs of stress or tension. He /she is open and accessible to the environment. The child expresses self-confidence and self-assurance

The Involvement scale focuses on the extent to which pupils are operating to their full capabilities. In particular it refers to whether the child is focused, engaged and interested in various activities.

Level	Wellbeing	Signals
1.	Extremely low	Activity is simple, repetitive and passive. The child seems absent and displays no energy. They may stare into space or look around to see what others are doing.
2.	Low	Frequently interrupted activity. The child will be engaged in the activity for some of the time they are observed, but there will be moments of non-activity when they will stare into space, or be distracted by what is going on around.
3.	Moderate	Mainly continuous activity. The child is busy with the activity but at a fairly routine level and there are few signs of real involvement. They make some progress with what they are doing but don't show much energy and concentration and can be easily distracted.
4.	High	Continuous activity with intense moments. The child's activity has intense moments and at all times they seem involved. They are not easily distracted.
5.	Extremely high	The child shows continuous and intense activity revealing the greatest involvement. They are concentrated, creative, energetic and persistent throughout nearly all the observed period.

How and when to use the scales

You are recommended to use the scales during periods of observation when the children are engaged in unsupported play, and repeat these at agreed intervals. Of course you would be likely to use the scales more frequently to track the progress of children causing concern. The use of the scales also means that you can track children's wellbeing and involvement alongside progress in their academic attainment, although as I have already said the two are intrinsically linked.

You should observe children as a small group or individually for a period of approximately two minutes each time, then give a score for wellbeing and/or involvement. It is thought that unless pupils are operating at 4 or 5, their learning will be limited. However, it is natural for levels of wellbeing and involvement to fluctuate throughout the day and it is therefore unrealistic to expect children to operate at levels 4 or 5 at all times. If you have a large number of children who are performing at a low level on this assessment, you might want to look at this helpful list of ten action points for looking at your provision, which have been devised by The Research Centre for Experiential Education (RCEE):

1. *Rearrange the classroom in appealing corners or areas.*
2. *Check the content of the areas and make them more challenging.*
3. *Introduce new and unconventional materials and activities.*
4. *Identify children's interests and offer activities that meet these.*
5. *Support activities by stimulating inputs.*
6. *Widen the possibilities for free initiative and support them with sound agreements.*
7. *Improve the quality of the relations amongst children and between children and teacher(s).*
8. *Introduce activities that help children to explore the world of behaviour, feelings and values.*
9. *Identify children with emotional problems and work out sustaining interventions.*
10. *Identify children with developmental needs and work out interventions that engender involvement.*

(www.earlylearninghq.org.uk/earlylearninghq-blog/the-leuven-well-being-and-involvement-scales)

In this chapter, I am suggesting that in using the EYFS criteria for learning, including the CEL (Characteristics of Effective Learning), we should be aware of children's sense of wellbeing and self-esteem. This will be evident in their ability to concentrate and focus on activities and to play and learn independently. One way of monitoring this is to use the Leuven Scales.

3 Effective assessment for learning

Assessment plays an important part in helping parents, carers and practitioners to recognise children's progress, understand their needs, and to plan activities and support. Ongoing assessment (also known as formative assessment) is an integral part of the learning and development process. It involves practitioners observing children to understand their level of achievement, interests and learning styles, and to then shape learning experiences for each child reflecting those observations. In their interactions with children, practitioners should respond to their own day-to-day observations about children's progress, and observations that parents and carers share.

(Statutory Framework for the Early Years Foundation Stage (EYFS); DfE; 2012)

In chapters 3 and 4, I'll begin to explore some ways of collecting evidence of learning, through both progress (how much the child has learned since the last assessment), and achievement (how each child is doing against national, local or school/setting expectations). This is usually referred to as 'formative', 'continuous' or 'ongoing' assessment. The focus will be on ways of collecting and presenting information that will allow you and your managers to interpret and understand what is going on, and to ensure that you can identify next steps in learning for each child.

Of course, as you work, you will need to reassess your children and reflect on what you see in your environment and teaching as the children's skills develop.

Observing and responding to children's learning

There are many ways of assessing what is going on in your setting, and they all take time! However, this time has to be found, or your planning will be wasted, as you won't know whether your planning has actually engaged any child, let alone helped them to make progress. Effective practitioners assess what is going on in many ways, and one of the most effective is to observe, and then respond to what you see – observation on its own is of no use if it doesn't make you respond!

Here is the 'Observe, assess, plan' process from Development Matters (Early Education; 2012). My amplification of the process follows.

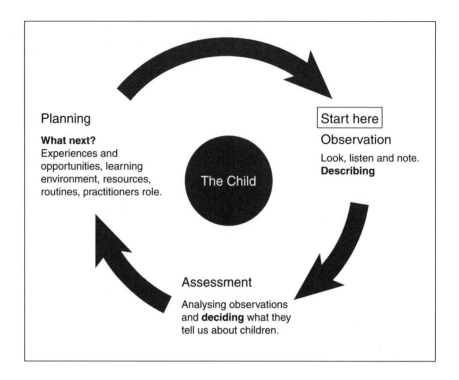

Planning

What next?
Experiences and
opportunities, learning
environment, resources,
routines, practitioners role.

The Child

Start here
Observation

Look, listen and note.
Describing

Assessment

Analysing observations
and **deciding** what they
tell us about children.

Observing

Adults take time to 'plan themselves out of activities' so that they can observe the children,
track their interests, their preferred areas of play and how they are thinking. Are children
developing problem-solving skills? Do they stick at a task until it is done? Do they give up
when things become difficult? Do they ask for help before trying something themselves?
During any period of observation, if adults feel it is appropriate, they can engage with
children in their play and exploration to further investigate their creative and shared
thinking processes through discussion and 'sustained shared thinking.'

Developing

Once you have got a good idea of the sorts of strategies your children are using in their
independent play and social interactions, then as adults, you can use modelling, scaffolding
and questioning strategies to extend children's thinking. Using our knowledge of children's
interests to support the context of the scenarios we create, will ensure that the children are
more likely to engage and learn.

Enhancing

Once children are aware of different strategies for thinking, it is up to the adults to provide
open-ended tasks that encourage children to think for themselves. Through 'sustained

shared thinking' – *'the adult being aware of the child's interests and understanding, and the adult and child together developing an idea or skill'; Marion Dowling* – adults can help children to 'think differently' or 'think creatively', which will help children to focus their thinking.

Reflecting

Regular reflection is crucial in all aspects of practice. Adults need to reflect on the ways the strategies that they are putting into place are having an impact on children. They also need to encourage the children to reflect on what they have learned about different ways of thinking. Making space for thinking and talking about thinking is essential, and all too rare in many Early Years settings!

Ambiguity, open questions and open situations

When it comes to developing creative and sustained thinkers, a good 'dollop' of ambiguity, also referred to as 'open-ended' activities, questions and situations, can hold the key to high quality learning. Although in some aspects of Early Years development children need very clear guidance and firm structure, it is always good to have an element of your practice and provision that will enable children to draw on their own experiences to form a conclusion – thinking creatively.

This can come in the form of your responses when children ask you for guidance and support. Rather than saying 'do it this way' or 'try that' you could answer their question with another question to get them thinking: 'What do you think would happen if . . .' 'I am not sure, how could we find out?' Sometimes they will have an idea and sometimes they won't – be patient, keep offering opportunities for them to expand their thinking, and model being a thinker yourself.

But ambiguity isn't just limited to asking questions; open-ended resources and activities that rely on children's creativity and imagination will promote higher-order thinking skills. For example, in your small world area a cow will always be a cow, but a wooden block can be anything, depending on whose hand it is in, the time of day, and current interests. Ambiguous, open-ended resources are a must in every area of provision. Such play is often referred to as heuristic play – play that enables children to discover or learn something for themselves, and because it uses natural, open-ended resources.

Resources for this sort of open-ended play could include:

Smaller objects such as: lengths of ribbon/string/lace, logs, twigs, wood slices, shells, polished stones, bottle corks, pine cones, nuts and bolts, paper clips, and fasteners, large wooden beads, buttons of all sorts and sizes, plastic food trays, lolly sticks, old CDs and DVDs, chestnuts and conkers, glass 'beads', cotton reels, feathers, leaves, marbles, sequins etc.

Larger items such as: logs, planks, rope, crates, guttering and drainpipes, garden boxes, barrows and carts, shower curtains, old sheets and blankets, bubble wrap, tarpaulins, tyres, cable reels etc.

And for joining and fixing: clothes pegs, bulldog clips, duct tape, masking tape, cable ties etc.
(Treasure Baskets and Heuristic Play; Sally Featherstone; Featherstone Education; 2013)

However, as well as being a great aid to learning, ambiguity and openness can also be a bit daunting for some children (and some adults too), especially if they are not used to thinking for themselves. An effective questioning environment is not just about how effectively the team can model thinking skills or how many open-ended resources you can provide. For these strategies to work, the children have to:

- **feel confident** enough to 'have a go' and be able to express what they are feeling and what they are thinking.

- **have the language** to be able to explain their thinking in a way that someone else can understand, talk about what they have done and begin to plan what they might do next.

- **show a level of imagination and creativity** in their talk and play. A good imagination is a very useful tool to a creative thinker.

- **demonstrate motivation and an eagerness to learn**. Even if it is only in the subjects that really interest them. If they haven't got an eagerness to find out then they are unlikely to stick with a problem until its resolution.

During such open-ended activities, adults are much more able to give time to observation of children's learning, as the children will be less reliant on adult support, using the adults as a resource, not a leader.

The role of the adult

Children will learn some of these skills through their individual experiences within the environment, but their progress will be significantly enhanced by the effective support and role models of the adults within this 'high quality learning environment'. As adult 'facilitators of thinking' we need to actively seek out opportunities to challenge and extend children's thinking. We can do this by creating activities and areas of provision to encourage creative thinking, while ensuring that children feel valued and supported, even when they feel that things are going wrong.

In her book on supporting sustained shared thinking, Marion Dowling has produced a set of prompts for the role of the adult in promoting the idea of 'sustained shared thinking'. They show that adults can use both verbal and non-verbal communications to develop positive interactions, assisting in the development of children's thinking skills. An example of what might be said has been added to each of the prompts. Marion Dowling says that adults need to:

- **Tune in**

  Kay approaches a group of three children playing outside on the climbing frame. She stands and watches for a moment to 'tune in' to what is happening.

- **Show genuine interest**

  Kay approaches the climbing frame and watches as the children continue their attempt to hoist up a bucket of water to the top platform of the frame, using a rope. She takes a photo and then asks them what is happening.

- **Respect children's own decisions and choices**

  Bren says 'We're trying to get water to pour on the baddies!'

- **Invite children to elaborate**

  'How are you doing that?'

  'We got the bucket but it fell off. Jenny helped us. She's good at knots.'

- **Recap**

  'So, you tied the bucket on the rope, but the knot didn't work very well so you asked Jenny to help. That sounds like a very good plan, is it working?'

- **Offer personal experience**

  'Can you remember when we went to the castle and saw the hole over the gate there for pouring things on baddies?'

- **Clarify ideas**

  'How are you going to pour the water out and make sure it goes on the baddies and not on your friends?'

- **Remind**

  'Remember that your ideas and plans must be safe for everyone.'

- **Use specific praise**

  'Those were very good ideas, I really like Rosie's idea of putting a notice up, so the water doesn't go on your friends.'

- **Offer an alternative viewpoint**

  'How do you think the baddies will feel when they get wet?'

- **Speculate**

  'I wonder if the baddies will see what you are doing and think of a plan too?'

So, the role of the adult is complex and pivotal in ensuring successful outcomes, but how do you manage when you don't have enough adults to respond to every need? Effective Early Year practitioners work very hard, but they can't be everywhere!

A risk-free environment

Often (usually) in periods of continuous provision (see page 36), children will opt for the activity or task that they find easiest. Easy tasks that involve very little challenge need very few thinking strategies and result in very low-level engagement. To help boost opportunities for children to develop their thinking we need to 'pepper' our provision, indoors and out with open-ended resources that allow children to explore cause and effect through trial and error. It is these processes particularly that help to encourage creative thinking both as an individual and as a group.

Because the resources have a high level of ambiguity, different children will use them in different ways, but they will still be exploring the same concepts. If you put a toy cat up a tree and ask the children how to get it down, once the cat has been rescued the problem has been solved. Once one solution has been reached for a specific scenario, the children are not inclined to look for an alternative. If, on the other hand, you create less prescriptive, more open-ended opportunities, then the possibilities for investigation and re-investigation are endless as children select and combine resources in different ways.

A good 'thinking environment' should be stimulating to children with a wide selection of materials that encourage exploration and investigation. There will be long uninterrupted periods of continuous provision that will allow children time to engage, play, investigate and talk. It should have a great emphasis on a play-based approach rather than an 'activity-based' approach where the outcomes and the process have already been predetermined. This approach will also use children's own work in displays as a way of praising their achievement and inspiring them and others to 'have a go'.

Adults will be enthusiastic supporters of children's learning and will take time to observe, listen and record not just what children are learning, but how they are learning it. They will also constantly look for opportunities to question, model and scaffold strategies and ideas. Children should really feel valued and not under pressure to provide 'quick' answers. Good thinking takes time. A good thinker is a creative thinker, so a good thinking environment will have lots of open-ended opportunities to be creative and to make links to previous learning. It will provide challenge and moments of reflection, not to mention a healthy dose of ambiguity!

Integral to teaching is how practitioners assess what children know, understand and can do as well as take account of their interests and dispositions to learning (characteristics of effective learning), and use this information to plan children's next steps in learning and monitor their progress.

(Evaluation schedule for inspections of registered early years provision Guidance and grade descriptors; Ofsted; 2014)

Peer work

A useful strategy for success is creating opportunities for children to work together to learn from and model for each other. Talking to someone else is a great way of getting ideas straight in your own head and getting someone else's opinion on whether your ideas will work or not. Usually in Early Years this type of peer work needs support and guidance from an adult, especially when it comes to the type of questioning and language that the children might use in discussion with each other.

Through really effective collaborative discussion with their peers, children can learn to:

- Ask questions that are related to the discussion (not always easy).
- Develop their own ideas rather than just focusing resolutely to the first point they made.
- Explain 'why' they think what they think.
- Learn not only to be quiet when other people are speaking, but actually listen to what they are saying and (sometimes) comment on it.
- Even possibly change their idea based on what they find out (and not just because their friend had a different idea!).

Planned 'thinking times', when children are given scenarios to think about and problems to solve, can be useful, but only if you aim to create a permanent 'thinking environment' where key thinking skills are promoted and enhanced at all times.

An environment based on assessment

Our quest for 'outstanding practice' must start with the learning environment that we create for our children. When it comes to what we have and where we have it, then nothing should be left to chance.

Our entire space should be informed by assessment. I am not talking about what we put on the shelves in the areas that we create. I am talking about the areas themselves. However small or inconvenient your space may be, how it looks and is organised should bear a direct relationship to the strengths and areas for development that you have identified through regular assessment. The needs of children change over time as they grow and develop, and so should the space that you create for them. How your space looks in September on point of entry should be completely different from how it will look in July when the children are getting ready to move on.

Tracking and documenting how you have created an environment based on assessment is a great way of showing the links you are making between play and learning. It is the first step on the audit trail you create as evidence of high-level opportunities for attainment outside and within direct teaching. Formative assessment (intended to 'inform' practice) is now part of every practitioner's working day – taking photos, making observations, making jottings of what children say. This information must be used or assessment time is wasted. There should be an automatic feedback loop, which enables you to adjust your provision in the light of what you see, hear and feel during your observations.

4 Summative assessment: Gap and Strength Analysis (GSA)

Summative assessment

The EYFS requires early years practitioners to review children's progress and share a summary with parents at two points:

- *in the prime areas between the ages of 24 and 36 months*
- *and at the end of the EYFS in the EYFS Profile.*

Development Matters might be used by early years settings throughout the EYFS as a guide to making best-fit judgements about whether a child is showing typical development for their age, may be at risk of delay or is ahead for their age. Summative assessment supports information sharing with parents, colleagues and other settings.

(Development Matters; Early Education; 2012)

Using the assessment information you have collected is a vital part of your accountability – to your team, to parents, managers, inspectors and of course, to the children themselves. In this chapter I'll unpack the ways in which you can use your formative assessment, particularly in Reception, to make summative assessments, and present these in a way that others can understand, and which helps you to identify the way forward for your group.

You will usually carry out a summative assessment, which pulls together all your observations and other information about each child, at least three times a year. These major summative assessments, use assessment information 'summed up' in:

- Late September/October (at point of entry, relying on the information provided by a previous practitioner and the parents, and your initial observations of the child in their new setting)
- December
- Sometime between Easter and the end of the Summer term.

As well as informing your practice these assessments will form the basis for your reports to parents at the end of each year, for the Two Year Old Assessment:

The revised EYFS requires that parents and carers must be supplied with a short written summary of their child's development in the three prime learning and development areas of the

EYFS: Personal, Social and Emotional Development; Physical Development; Communication and Language. This summary must be provided when the child is aged between 24–36 months.

and at the end the final term in Reception for completing the Early Years Foundation Stage Profile (EYFSP):

In the final term of the year in which the child reaches age five, and no later than 30 June in that term, the EYFS Profile must be completed for each child.

(Statutory Framework for the EYFS; DfE; 2012)

Between these major assessments you will 'tweak' and 'enhance' your space, based on your ongoing daily assessments and observations.

Looking at all this information and its implications must impact on how you change your space in a fairly significant way at least three times a year in response to the information that you have collected and interpreted, and of course this interpretation is the central part of the process – useful information ceases to be useful if it is not used!

Gap and strength analysis (GSA)

Inspectors should evaluate how well leaders use formative and summative assessment to ensure that pupils, teachers and parents know if pupils are achieving the expected standard or if they need to catch up. Inspectors should consider how well:

- *assessment information, including test results, is used by leaders and governors to improve teaching and the curriculum.*

(The School Inspection Handbook; Ofsted; 2015)

Following every summative assessment that you carry out, I would suggest that you create a GSA (Gap and Strength Analysis). This will be your blueprint for mapping your space. A GSA is exactly what it sounds like. It identifies where your biggest learning gaps are and also where your children have areas of strength. You will use the information to help you to plug the gaps and create challenge where there are areas of strength. Your GSA will help you to create an appropriate learning environment. It also helps you to demonstrate how you can achieve high-level attainment in Foundation Stage, which as we know, can be tricky!

So, what to do and how to do it. . .

A GSA uses the information that you gain from your summative assessment to show where the *greatest areas of need and strength are within your cohort*. You should then make sure that the environment and provision that you put in place directly reflects the needs that you have identified. Where there are areas of particular strength then you would ensure that you planned explicit and implicit challenge. So, if talk or physical development shows up as a need then I would expect to see lots more areas of the environment and resources in place to support that development. There is no point having a 'maths' and 'handwriting' area with no one in it, when that space could be given over to providing more learning opportunities in an area of identified need.

You will fill in your GSA three times a year following summative assessment. This will probably be October, December and April. If you have a constantly changing cohort (like playgroup or day nursery) then you would carry out a GSA every three months and 'tweak' your environment in response to any specific need that you have identified in the interim.

NB: This is an example of a Reception Gap Analysis using Autumn 2 summative assessment. In this particular setting, and because there are no children who are performing above the expected level for their age, this is a pure Gap Analysis.

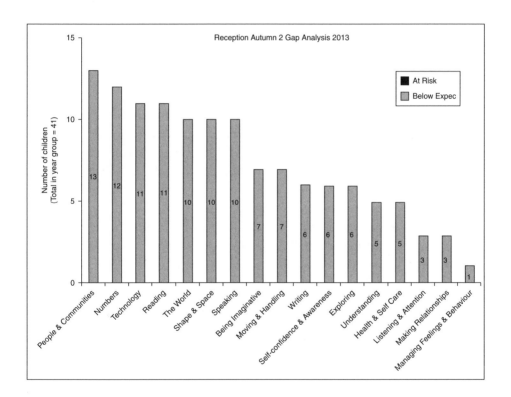

Step 1

Once you have completed your assessment, you need to identify the children who are performing below the age-related expectation in each of the prime and specific areas of learning and development. When I complete a GSA with a setting I always encourage them to include any children who have just tipped into the expected age band, as they are emergent learners and still at risk of not meeting the expectations.

As in the example included here, some areas, like 'People and Communities' can often score highly because young children often have limited knowledge and experience of other people and communities outside their own. Their knowledge in this area will grow through the experiences that you give them and this takes time. It is still worth asking the question how you make your children aware of people and communities. Do you have to wait until the 'People that help us' topic title comes along, or do you have a really good range of stories, songs, games etc. that you use consistently?

One setting I was working with got a very similar result from their GSA and decided to use some of their space to create a 'Multicultural area'. This area was full of multicultural costumes, artefacts and images. The children used the area a lot and the team felt that it was therefore having impact. However, when we watched and listened to what the children were actually doing in the area during continuous provision, it had very little to do with other cultures and a great deal to do with familiar domestic role play. When an adult was working in the space, then it was a different story which shows we really need to focus on what the children will do when there is *no* adult there, as that is when learning is most at risk.

Step 2

Using your same assessment, identify the children who are performing above the expected age-related score in each of the prime and specific areas of learning and development. These children are demonstrating a high level of capability and you need to ensure that when you move on to actually 'stock' your continuous provision that you have catered for their needs with challenging and open-ended resources.

Of course the levels of attainment on entry will affect the number of children at each expected point. These 'expected levels' are usually agreed using the Unique Child column in Development Matters, which gives general statements for each of the age bands in the EYFS. Some settings will have a lot of children who start the year below expectations, some will have a significant number of children who start the year above the expectation at point of entry. As always in the Early Years, you work with what you've got! The important thing is that you show that you are using assessment to inform your planning, from the environment you create, right through to your direct teaching.

Step 3

Once you have gathered all of this lovely data, the best thing to do with it is to make a graph. Why a graph? Well, because everybody loves a graph (especially senior management and Ofsted) and you want your data to be presented in the most visual and user-friendly way possible. Here is an example of a Reception class GSA following their second summative assessment in December.

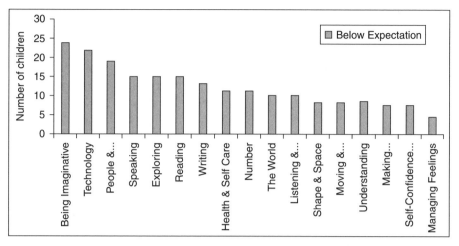

Foundation Stage 2 Gap and Strength Analysis; December

There are 27 children in the class, so as you can see, some of the gaps are quite significant, for example:

In 'Being Imaginative', 24 children are below expectations for their age

In 'Technology' 22 children are below expectations for their age

And in 'People & Communities' 19 children are below expectations for their age.

This is worrying, and the practitioners in this setting need to find out what is going on and decide what to do.

Step 4

The next step in your setting would be to interpret your own data and then apply what you have found to your learning environment. This is the interesting and sometimes tricky bit! If nothing else, your GSA should get you and your team talking about the needs you have identified and how you are going to tackle them. If we take this GSA as an example, I would want to agree with my team what constituted a significant 'gap' that might need some significant 'tackling' and what was more of a day-to-day need that could be tackled on an individual level. Significant gaps like this need careful intervention, and putting them right sometimes indicates just as much change for the adults as it does for the children.

Obviously, the greatest need identified here is 'Being Imaginative' with 24 of the 27 children not meeting the age-related expectation. Also, as we work along the graph we can see that in all areas up to 'Heath and Self Care', 50 percent or more of the class are showing a need. The left-hand third of the graph shows us our most significant gaps. Beyond 'Health and Self Care' you can see that the proportion moves down to about a third, which is still a significant number, gradually decreasing until we get to 'Managing Feelings', where there are only two children. The chances are that you are going to be well aware of who <u>those</u> two are, and will already have something in place to help, support and manage their development! It would be up to your practitioner team, with the support of your management team, to make a judgement call on what you/they felt would constitute a 'significant gap' and that is where you would start.

Step 5

The next exercise can be a bit of a 'brain acher', but it is well worth the effort. You have got your lovely visually pleasing graph, you are now going to interpret that graph and record your thoughts on paper. This will form the basis of your very own Environment Plan, which is going to become your ongoing record of the process. You will formally update it every time you do a summative assessment, and then use it as part of your evidence trail of progress.

For the areas that you have identified as being 'significant gaps' you should complete a sheet that looks something like this:

Class: Reception GSA Assessment Autumn 2	Focus areas for development:
	Priority Areas 1 (50% or more below expectations): Being Imaginative, Technology, People & Communities **Priority Areas 2 (30% – 50% below expectations):** Speaking, Exploring Media & Materials; Reading
Focus areas	**Resources needed**

At the top right of the sheet you record the areas of learning and development that you are focusing on. Then in the space below it you are going to list all of the areas of provision (focus areas) or learning opportunities that you think have the most potential to help you to fill that gap.

Now fill in the left hand column with the areas of provision where you think you need to make changes or do something different to raise attainment and involvement. Any area of provision can have any focus when there is an adult in it to direct the learning, so *focus your thinking particularly on continuous provision* – particularly those areas where there is less likely to be an adult.

On the right-hand side you can then list the resources, equipment and training that you think you might need to help you to support the need identified by assessment. The great thing about this sheet is that when you hand in a list of resources to be signed off by the headteacher (or whoever holds the power!) everything you have identified has been linked directly to assessment and doesn't look like you just picked it out of the catalogue because you liked the look of it – so who could refuse?

When you have really thought about what you need, your list may look something like this. In this example, the practitioners feel that if they can combine the resource list so it covers more than one of the priority areas of need, they may be more likely to get what they need:

Class: Reception GSA Assessment Autumn 2	Focus areas for development: **Priority Areas 1 (50% or more below expectations):** Being Imaginative, Technology, People & Communities **Priority Areas 2 (30% – 50% below expectations):** Speaking, Exploring Media & Materials, Reading
Focus areas	**Resources needed**
We want to improve children's ability to be imaginative when they are NOT with an adult, so the resources will be used in both adult led and child initiated activities, across these areas: • the shared art area • outside • small world • role play • book corner	• Re-vamp the **outside 'stage' area** to include music and dance. • **Black/whiteboards** and other vertical surfaces for paint, chalk, clay, mud in and out of doors. • Resources for **independent den building** – canes, clips, cable ties, plastic and fabric sheets. • **A curtain rail round the underneath of the big climbing frame** so we can put shower curtains up and make an enclosed space for imaginative play. • More resources for **small world play** to encourage imaginative play and storytelling – play people vehicles and characters, puppets, TV and DVD characters. • **Backgrounds and drapes** to encourage creativity. • Some **new and imaginative picture books**, including more books with **black and ethnic characters**, more poetry and rhyme, finger puppets, pictures of the community, and of other people. • **Kindles, dictaphones, talking tins, talking photo albums**, telephones, painting/drawing programs for the IWB for children to use. • Support for more **visits** to theatres, galleries, artists studios and the local community. • **Visitors** – theatre, music, artists in residence. • **A new craft trolley** for our shared art area, with a better range of materials and media, so children can choose their own resources without having to ask the adults. • **A small allocation of money for local buying** (at the pound shop, garden centre, B&Q, charity shops), so we can adapt the role play area to suit the emerging interests of the children.
Most of the things we need will be useful for both priorities 1 and 2, particularly to encourage creativity and exploring media.	

The 'how' question

If the graph on page 29 belonged to my setting then I would take each 'gap' in turn and ask the team to list all of the areas of provision that they thought would help to fill that gap. Our most pressing area is 'Being Imaginative'. The majority of the children are not able to show or evidence that they have or are using an expected level of imagination. I will, of course, take this information into account when I am thinking about planning my direct teaching, focused work and modelling. But, as the children are going to spend a significant part of their time in areas of continuous provision, we need to identify which areas of learning and development we think will most effectively promote learning around 'Being Imaginative' *without* an adult. When I carried out this exercise with the team who produced the original data, this is what they said:

Area : Being imaginative
Areas that promote facilitation:

- role play

- small world

- construction

- outdoor

- malleable materials.

Then they stopped and said: 'Is this a trick? Won't we need to look at every area?' So we started again by asking the 'how' question.

The 'how' question is the most crucial in this process, so when we are trying to 'feed' and extend the imagination of children who have very little, how will enhancing these areas actually give children what they need? You can provide the most amazing role play in the world, but just putting a child into it will not increase their imagination, as they will only be able to use the creativity and imagination they already have. In truth all the areas they identified are great for consolidating whatever level of imagination children have. What they are not great for (particularly in the absence of an adult) is feeding and enhancing that imagination.

So, we started our list again! This time we were looking for opportunities to feed imagination. The first question this time was: *How do we feed children's imaginations?* – and this is the new list that the team came up with:

- we tell them stories
- we look at pictures and books together
- we give them 'real' experiences with objects and materials
- we take them on trips and visits
- we invite visitors to come and meet the children

- we sing songs together
- we watch videos
- we talk!

This helped them enormously in filling in the form, as many of the things they needed could be used right across the setting, indoors and outside, and in adult led sessions as well as during continuous provision. The other thing was that most of the resources they suggested would support development in all the areas of concern, right across the spectrum.

The big question now is how can we enhance our environment in each of these areas so that children will have access *and* develop their imaginative ability in the absence of an adult? When you and your team start thinking about assessment in this 'broad sweep' way it can really focus your judgments and help to create greater team coherence.

This chapter has unpacked the process of turning formative assessment into summative assessment, using information about individual children to construct charts and diagrams for use by others and by the team, particularly to identify and address gaps and needs.

5 Effective provision

A stimulating learning environment, which offers high quality continuous provision is key to supporting children's learning and development. Now could be a good time to 'Spring Clean' the learning provision, maintaining and developing areas which are well used by children, and reflecting on those areas which seem to engage children less. Are there too many resources, or too few? Is the area of provision in the right place, or is it too noisy or too quiet? Do practitioners spend too much or too little time in the area?

Ongoing plans will include experiences and opportunities, which enhance areas of provision.

(Preparing for the new EYFS; Foundation Years; 2012)

In this chapter I'll begin to unpack the difference between the types of provision in an Early Years setting. We are all familiar with what I have referred to as 'basic provision', the backbone of every setting, and the resources that are expected in each one – bricks, sand, water, books, soft toys, paint, a home corner etc. These have been fixed elements of every Nursery and Reception class for many years, mostly unchanged since the concept of Nursery education was invented. Children have free access to these activities and they stay the same for the whole time the child spends in the setting, – the same books, the same resources in the sand and water etc. – and children access these in periods of free choice, with little or no intervention from adults.

However, this 'free-access' play has more recently been enhanced by the concept of continuous provision, with resources, equipment and activities in each area carefully matched to the age and stage of development of the children in the group. Activities and equipment change to help with skills development and to maintain children's interest by responding to what they enjoy and are captivated by at the moment.

In short, for me...

- **Basic provision** – resources linked to 'expected' ages and stages of development or historical knowledge of cohorts.

- **Continous provision** – resources linked to current assessment that have been levelled to match the attainment and learning preferences of your current cohort.

- **Enhanced provision (object or prompt)** – areas of provision that have been enhanced with objects or prompts that support an interest or encourage investigation and questioning.

- **Enhanced provision (skill)** – areas that have been enhanced with resources to support the teaching of a specific skill or concept. These resources will have been levelled in accordance with current assessment and 'dressed' for interest and engagement.

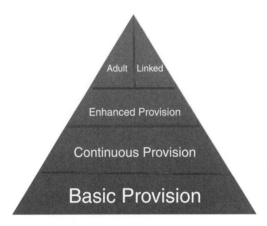

The provision pyramid

Basic provision

Basic provision comes at the bottom of the provision pyramid because it is the broadest and simplest provision that we provide for children. At its most 'basic', basic provision is just putting out in the environment the only resources that we have! In settings that have a range of resources at their disposal, basic provision is the provision that you provide for children, which is not linked directly to your assessment of their strengths, needs or learning preferences. This type of provision would include sand and water, brick play, simple dressing up, books and table-top toys, paint, construction sets, wheeled toys etc.

What you set out for your basic provision is often linked to the general age-related expectations for children. You are most likely to set up basic provision in a point of entry environment where you want children to have interesting and familiar resources to support their transition into your environment. Once you have carried out your first set of assessments, you can begin to apply that knowledge to your environment and areas of provision that exist within it. At this point you will be moving your provision to the next level on the pyramid – continuous provision.

Continuous provision

Well-planned continuous provision can be an absolute gift when it comes to raising the attainment of children through active learning and high-level engagement. Badly-planned continuous provision, on the other hand, can be a curse that promotes low-level engagement and low-level attainment – so what is the secret of good continuous provision?

Continuous provision is *not* just the resources that you have out all of the time. The purpose of continuous provision is to enhance basic provision resources so they better meet the needs and interests of individuals or groups of children. Continuous provision has been enhanced by the adults following observations of the children, and is usually provided to be accessed without the support of an adult. Continuous provision should continue the provision for learning in the absence of an adult rather than just support low-level engagement.

In any area where you put a range of resources and a group of children there will be potential to develop those children's skills in personal interaction and exploration, but unless those resources have been carefully selected to meet the development needs of those specific children, the learning potential is limited and greatly left to chance. When children are given the opportunity to 'choose' they tend to pick things that they like and know that they can do. How many times have you commented that the same children are in the construction area creating the same sorts of models, and that group of girls are back at the mark-making table drawing and colouring?

We can also mistake compliance with engagement and progress, and this can be a fatal error. There will be lots of children who are very happy to stay in an area of the provision for sustained periods of time. They will comply with the agreed behaviour code and will often be prolific in their output. But, if we look at what they have produced and then ask ourselves if it shows challenge and learning, or just low-level consolidation of a skill that they already had, then we are likely to see that it is the latter. Where this is the case, we are not continuing the provision for learning but 'holding' children until an adult gets to them and boosts their progress with their input. If you pause to consider the length of time some children spend in this level of provision without adult input, then this has huge implications for potential lack of progress in skills. If your continuous provision is just a selection of resources linked to a general area of development, then when a child is playing there, their opportunities for learning are limited.

Continuous provision linked to assessment

Even in freely accessed 'adult free' continuous provision, the resources and organisation of each area of your room should be levelled to meet the particular needs of the children in your current cohort. As well as providing opportunities for exploration and discovery, your continuous provision *must be* linked to assessment. If activities are going to be available all the time, and children are going to access them with limited adult input, they *must* be structured around their development needs and dressed to reflect their interests.

How well could you answer the following questions about your basic continuous provision?

- Could you show me your assessment, and how you have linked it to specific resources?
- Could you stand in front of each area of continuous provision in your setting, and explain how everything in that area is directly linked to your observation and assessment of your children?
- Does the size of the areas of continuous provision reflect the needs of your cohort? If you have children who need to develop language and talk skills, have you significantly increased the size of those areas?
- Have you levelled your continuous provision, linked to assessment so that you can show which resources have been linked to the development of high, middle and low achievers in that area?

An example – Developing mark making to meet the needs of different groups

If we were standing in front of your mark-making area, could you show me how you had set that space up to reflect the mark-making development of your current cohort? Have you got resources in place that are specifically aimed at each stage of their mark-making development?

If you have a range of development, then you will need to provide a range of resources that meet the needs and stages of mark-making development of each group of children.

You might want to consider if you need a mark-making area at all. Children will tend to mark make more often when resources are placed throughout provision rather than just in one spot.

The palmar grip

When children first begin to mark make they are not doing it to necessarily convey meaning, they are doing it because they can, and they find mark making fascinating. We need to capitalise on children's desire to make marks, as well as accurately assess their physical mark-making development. Once we are aware of where they are, then we can ensure that our environment and planning will support their further development.

By the time they enter your setting, most children will have already developed a grasp that allows them to hold something tight without dropping it. Their grasp is formed by wrapping their fingers around the object, making a fist, with the object held in the palm. This is known as the 'palmar grip'.

At this stage you will need to provide lots of chubby, easy-to-hold mark makers and endless surfaces for mark making, preferably in big sizes, and not just paper, but whiteboards, blackboards, walls and tables!

The shoulder pivot

Often at this stage the child will have a fairly stiff wrist and a straight elbow, with most of the movement coming from the shoulder. The marks that a child at this stage of development can make will be at the maximum range, so they are likely to be long and straight or large and circular as the child's range of movement is restricted to the strongest muscle group they have available – their shoulder – and usually still with the mark maker in a palmar grip.

As part of your assessment for mark making are you looking for children who are pivoting from the shoulder with this palmar supinate grasp? What are the implications for your mark-making resources and surfaces? Within your planning for adult-led activities, can you show how you have grouped children for specific interventions and also how you will support their mark-making development during periods of child-led learning or continuous provision?

Children at this stage need plenty of space where they can practise their shoulder pivot. They will also need to continue with easy-to-hold mark makers. At this stage they will appreciate such activities as brushing and mopping, scribbling on interactive whiteboards, and spraying foam across the ground or on tree trunks or walls.

Upper body work out

Once we have established that we are concentrating on developing children's shoulder movement and their sense of balance then we would plan for fixed or permanent structures in our environment to support this movement as well as enhancements and activities to develop it.

The activities that we plan will involve the use of the shoulder pivot on both horizontal and vertical surfaces. The activities will encourage the children to reach and stretch as well as use the full circular motion of their shoulder joint. You should engage children at this stage of development in this type of activity on a daily basis, so set up your continuous provision to offer opportunities such as:

- washing walls
- painting with mops
- swing ball with a pair of tights
- lolly stick race tracks
- swing painting (tights and teabags)
- painting trees with shaving foam
- foam bike tracks
- big digging with sand and soil.

Elbow pivot

Once the muscles in the back, upper arms and shoulders begin to strengthen, then there is usually more movement further down the arm at the next point of pivot, the elbow.

As with a shoulder pivot, when you are assessing children's mark-making abilities and planning their next steps development then you need to know which children are at this stage and what you have purposefully put in your provision and planning to consolidate that skill and take them forward.

First of all you should split your children into 'emergent' and 'proficient' elbow pivoters because you will promote different activities for each. For 'emergent' children you really want to encourage them to use their full range of motion, making sure they bending their elbows. You are going to need lots of space for them to move their arms up and down as well as side to side across their body. Large rollers or brushes moved up and down on outside surfaces are not only good activities for developing the elbow pivot, they are going to contribute to consolidating the shoulder pivot.

A sweeping motion with a stiff outside brush is also good for this pivot. The children can have sweeping races through piles of leaves or create foam tracks on a rainy day with the aid of some washing-up liquid! Good old blackboard paint is a lifesaver here too. This isn't only for painting boards, you can also paint your walls and furniture. Children can develop an emergent elbow pivot by sawing wood with a hacksaw. Of course it is not the opportunity to develop their elbow pivot that will attract them to this activity, more the opportunity to get their hands on a saw. NB: Children need training and supervision when they are using woodwork tools.

For a more secure elbow pivot, you really want the children to develop that circular 'push/pull' movement with their upper and lower arm. There are lots of activities that you can do that involve a circular motion, both large and small. These can be as simple as drawing circles onto large sheets of sugar paper. Try doing this to music for an extra bit of inspiration.

You might also like to try activities such as:

- pulling their body up on ropes or a climbing wall
- ribbon or scarf twirling (they can pretend that the scarves are fire and that they are shooting it out of their hands)
- throwing and catching using their elbows to push the hand forward
- sawing wood
- making patterns in sand with lollipop sticks (turned on their side)
- sticking and pulling plungers from vertical and horizontal surfaces.

Wrist pivot

As the arm muscles and the sense of balance develop further then the pivot changes again, this time to allow an even smaller range of movement. This time the pivot moves to the wrist. The elbow often tucks into the side of the body and the shoulder movement is now minimal.

By the time that children reach the wrist pivot stage in their development their lower arms, upper arms and shoulders are all now well developed and their overall movement and balance tends to be far more fluid than it was when they first started out on this journey of development.

The wrist pivot stage is the one that children tend to stick with for the least amount of time before their pivot shifts again. Often with a wrist pivot comes a change in a child's grip from palmar supinate to digital pronate (digit meaning finger and pronate meaning to grasp with the palm turned down). When a child adopts a digital pronate grip they bed their wrist to nearly 45 degrees, grip their mark-making implement with three fingers and use their first finger to manipulate the end of their pencil. This is a clear sign that their stage of fine-motor manipulation is moving forward and also an indicator that we need to be looking out for and encouraging the next stage of development both in pivot and grip.

What might provision to support a wrist pivot look like?

When planning provision to support a developing wrist pivot we want to encourage the whole range of wrist movement. The wrist pivot itself is allowing the child a much more defined and small-scale range of movement. The movement range of the activities that you plan for a developing wrist pivot will be much smaller than what you have planned before. You might want to reduce everything in size to encourage the child to really focus on their development. Having a range of smaller working surfaces constantly available for the children to self select is always a good idea.

Any sort of threading or weaving activity is great for developing a wrist pivot. The thing about threading is that is has great benefits but can be dull, especially for some of those children who would rather be playing Ben 10 outside! It is not often that you will see those children whoop with joy at the sight of some plastic cotton reels!

Tip

Don't just think about which activities get the children flexing the right muscles in the right places, think about what is going to make them want to engage with that activity in the first place and how you can theme it around their interests.

To encourage a wrist pivot try:

- threading
- sewing
- dabbing with a sponge or brush
- popping pictures
- fishing game (or similar)
- splatter painting.

This example of levelling the skills needed for early mark making will help you to provide the right resources and opportunities for the right children. However, this does not mean that children who already have control of their shoulder pivot should never have a chance to play with foam on a blackboard wall!

The adult's role in continuous provision

It is important to understand that as soon as you engage with children in continuous provision then the play risks becoming at least 'adult influenced' if not adult led. Practitioners who watch, wait and sometimes even creep away so they don't demolish the play, are the ones who really are following the children! This sort of adult-led provision can have a very positive impact on children's engagement and attainment if done sensitively. It can also be very effective at sending learning off the rails and scattering children to the four corners of your setting (especially if you have a clipboard in your hand).

Judging if, when and how you intervene in children's play is not an exact science and no one gets it right all of the time. But, when you do it well, it allows you to observe, challenge, support and extend children's learning all based on the high-level engagement that you will get because they are at play.

Linked provision

'Linked provision' is a bit of a hybrid that I first used with a Reception setting to help them to get round their issue of hearing guided readers, without compromising their continuous provision. Since then I have worked on versions of it from Pre-School to Year One. An example of this sort of provision is Funky Fingers (page 112).

So what is linked provision? Well, the clue is in the name... It is provision that you link to a need that has been identified by observation or assessment, and I would run it as a short daily session – usually at the very beginning of the day.

Everyone is engaged in activities that are themed around the identified need. The same activities are repeated every day for a week and the children get to experience and repeat all of them. The children can choose which of the offered activities they join (apart from any involved in withdrawal sessions for language development, reading etc.)

How can you use it?

I have worked with settings that have used linked provision in a variety of ways. You could use it:

- **to reinforce** teaching and concepts from the week before
- **to support social development** – so lots of activities that involve turn taking or sharing
- **as a designated talk time**, where the children have been encouraged to work in large or small groups around particular aspects of talk
- **to teach new concepts** that will then be made available in continuous provision, so children learn how to play games like dominoes or lotto
- **to support** the development of fine and gross motor skill development
- **to focus** on problem solving or thinking skills
- **to work on** number recognition, number bonds, shape or measure.

Once you start the list seems endless!

A session of linked provision lasts anything between 10 and 20 minutes depending on the age of the children and their stage of development. Like continuous provision, linked provision *must* be activity based, child led, active and fun. Linked provision is *not* sitting

down at a table with a handwriting sheet, or sitting on the carpet with a whiteboard and pen. It is active and engaging!

During a session of linked provision, I wouldn't make all areas available. Ideally this would be great, but realistically it is just too difficult to manage and maintain. Set up 'key' areas or 'stations' that are linked to the subject you are focusing on and let the children work in those.

What is the role of the adult in linked provision?

In some settings, each adult has managed an 'activity' or 'area' especially when the link is to something like the rules of game play. Sometimes one adult has taken an overview of the provision while the other adult or adults have withdrawn children for interventions like speech and language support or reading. Be careful, because if you pull a child out of good continuous provision then you run a great risk of compromising their learning. The provision isn't continuous if you keep stopping it.

Because linked provision is a much shorter session, themed around a more specific focus and repeated across the week, children have multiple opportunities to revisit a concept in a variety of contexts. I would always have my linked provision sessions first thing, following self-registration. This also allows some time for any late-comers who then don't miss out on any direct input.

At the end of linked provision, I would then come to the carpet for a good old talk session, signposting of the day or a direct teaching session.

Linked provision is by no means an essential part of your day. It is just a strategy that I have used with lots of settings now that has not only solved some timetabling issues, but has had a significant impact on attainment.

So, just to recap. . .

Linked provision is a daily short session of play-based, child-led activities that have been planned around a specific area of need or consolidation that you have identified through observation and assessment. The role of the adult may change depending on the focus, but primarily they are there to facilitate, teach and support quality learning through play. Children will have the opportunity to experience and then re-visit key concepts across the week. Adults will have the opportunity to withdraw individual or groups of children for focused intervention or teaching.

Planning for continuous provision

Teaching should not be taken to imply a 'top down' or formal way of working. It is a broad term, which covers the many different ways in which adults help young children learn. It includes their interactions with children during planned and child-initiated play and activities: communicating and modelling language, showing, explaining, demonstrating, exploring ideas, encouraging, questioning, recalling, providing a narrative for what they are doing, facilitating and setting challenges. It takes account of the equipment they provide and the attention to the physical environment as well as the structure and routines of the day that establish expectations.

(Evaluation schedule for inspections of registered early years provision
Guidance and grade descriptors; Ofsted; 2014)

To be able to show what you are doing in your areas of continuous provision, you need to produce a weekly continuous provision plan. The problem with most continuous provision plans is that we spend ages writing them, but the objectives are unrealistic in terms of what children will actually do when they get into that provision space, and don't actually do what we write on the plan. The key question to ask yourself when you are planning is 'Will they do this when I am not there?' If the answer is 'no' or 'probably not', then you need to think again.

For example, lots of settings will put specific capacity objectives into their sand or water play continuous provision planning, such as:

- *'Children will fill containers to the given mark and compare'.*

Will they? Really? Or will they just stand and pour? Or just stand? Or get something else to play with?

Or mark making will make its way into continuous provision planning for the sand tray, with this sort of objective:

- *'Children will attempt to write the first letter of their name and then practise handwriting patterns using tools provided'.*

Hmmm, probably not!

These statements are not continuous provision plans, they are wishful adult focuses within an area of continuous provision. They are the focus you might want an adult to have when they visit children in play *if* they feel that the play they are observing would benefit from support, challenge or enhancement.

Of course, there will also be times when specific areas of continuous provision have been enhanced with a skill that you are focusing on or that contain an explicit challenge for the children to complete. You might, for example, have enhanced your creative area with a skills focus on printing or used your malleable materials areas to facilitate a

focus on reading. However, if you are not there, you can't be sure that the children will do what you would like them to! Be realistic.

Formats for planning

Your continuous provision plans need to contain enough information to be useful, without them taking 24 hours to write and read like *War and Peace*! So, what could they look like?

The first method of weekly planning that I use for continuous provision is the 'what', 'why' format. This is a simple overview of your continuous provision that would still need a bit of explanation if someone was using it to track attainment through continuous provision. It comprises a really simple grid where you list all of the areas of provision that you have created. Each area gets its own box. In the box under 'what' you would list what you had enhanced that area with this week. Under 'why' you would say why you have added that enhancement (assessment, skill, interest etc.). I always then do a very brief levelling of any enhancement that I had added to show differentiation. I also indicate any areas where I have added specific challenge.

This is an example of a teacher's planning using this format.

Book Corner

What? - Selection of books about space to enhance existing book basket, mark-making materials, key vocabulary cards around space to support children in their mark making.

Why? - To encourage children to make effective use of the book area and share books. Ask questions and enjoy familiar and unfamiliar texts. Support children's application of Ph2 and Ph3 phonemes around an area of specific interest.

> ### Deconstructed Role Play
>
> *What? - Remove crates tubes and planks and add cardboard boxes like we have had at the beginning of the year. Add other items such as talking telephones, fabric, saucepans anything to support some imagination.*
>
> *Why? Children very secure with the use of basic resources. Observation shows play is becoming very repetitive and language is low level. Open-ended resources will give more potential for the development of imagination with adult support*

The 'what' has been driven by assessment, the 'why' is a prompt for adults. Obviously, there is no guarantee that just because you put it there the children will access it in the way that you want them to, but if all adults are aware of what is there and why, it can help them to provide effective challenge and support when they visit the activity!

The second method of continuous provisions planning has a little more detail to it. My version looks like this.

Continuous Provision Plan   **Week Beginning:** (fill in date)

Area	Objective	Enhancement
Workshop and Creative	**AOL**: Mark Making **OBJ**: To attempt to mark make around own interests or following a prompt or stimulus **FOCUS**: To write an independent piece of work using appropriate pencil grip representing, sounds effectively	• Pictures and objects prompted by stimulus • Differentiated mark-making materials • CHALLENGE AREA
Construction	**AOL**: Physical Development - Personal, Social and Emotional **OBJ**: Build using levelled provision around interests or in response to a stimulus **FOCUS**: Initiate collaborative play, share ideas, adapt their work, use appropriate construction materials	• Differentiated construction kits (dexterity) • Stimulus linked to interest of target group (space) • Enlarged space to encourage collaboration
Malleable Materials	**AOL**: Mark Making **OBJ**: Children experience texture, opportunities for talk, cause and effect and changing states **FOCUS**: Develop gross and fine motor skills, letter recognition and formation	• Builder's tray • Gloop • Differentiated mark-making tools
Round Table	**AOL**: Mathematics - Physical Development **OBJ**: Development of dexterity through threading **FOCUS**: Fine motor dexterity, number recognition, matching, comparison, addition, counting back, awareness of time	• Thick and thin thread • Objects to thread (differentiated by size) • Mark-making materials • Sand timer • Numbers for reference and labelling • CHALLENGE AREA

On the table opposite the column 'Area' is not the area of learning and development, but the area in your setting. This is because you will often use an area of provision as a facilitator for another area of learning. So, you might be looking at 'Shape, space and measures' but in your construction area.

Under the 'Objective' column you are going to identify:

- the area of learning and development
- the objectives that your continuous provision in that area has been planned to support
- the focus for the adult (*if* required to enhance play).

In the 'Enhancement' column you will list any specific resources that you have added, any differentiation and any explicit challenges.

The next step in the process is to share this information with the adults who will be working in your space. The most obvious way to do that is to give them a copy of the planning – but with the best will in the world, that is a great deal of information to store in your head along with everything else that you have to think about, and practitioners are always looking for a solution to this problem.

Some settings now create adult 'prompt' cards that differentiate a particular skill focus that they have chosen to enhance an area of continuous provision with. There are many and various ways of doing this. It is really a question of what suits your team best. I have seen some settings use the 'WALT' and 'WILF' format for prompt cards for children. What I don't see very often (at all) are children in EYFS using 'WALT' and 'WILF' to plan and evaluate their own play and learning. If you are going to use prompt cards, then remember to audit their impact through observation. You don't want to spend your life creating laminated cards that no one reads!

> **WALT** *means* **We Are Learning To** … **WILF** *means* **What I'm Looking For** *as a point of reference so the children know the adults' criteria for success.*
>
> www.teachitprimary.co.uk

Something to consider

When adopting the techniques for managing and identifying learning detailed in this chapter, it is important to use them carefully and not allow them to 'rule' your provision and the children's activities. Practitioners working with younger children – those in Nursery provision, and in the early months of their Reception year – should use these techniques sparingly, and not allow them to overwhelm the environment for independent learning.

Planning for continuous provision, and making sure you have the best balance between 'child-led' and 'adult-led' activity is a complex task, and in outstanding provision, practitioners are expected to use their assessments to inform continuous provision as well as the more specific and targeted activities led or influenced by adults.

6 Pure and facilitative skills

Three areas are particularly crucial for igniting children's curiosity and enthusiasm for learning, and for building their capacity to learn, form relationships and thrive. These three areas, the prime areas, are:

- *communication and language;*
- *physical development; and*
- *personal, social and emotional development.*

(Statutory Framework for the EYFS; DfE; 2012)

In this chapter I introduce the idea of looking carefully at the 'basic provision' in your room, and unpacking the skills that children are developing as they play in that particular provision. I've used wet and dry sand as examples, to help you to understand the task of listing the skills. Once you have done this you will need to do the same thing with each of your areas, so you can use this work on identifying skills lists which can help you to plan activities targeted at children at different developmental levels.

One thing that will really help you and your team, especially with your planning for continuous provision, is to think about *why* we have the particular areas of provision that we have in Early Years. What skills can children learn when they are playing and learning in them? One way to allocate these skills is to start by dividing them into two groups, identifying which are the 'pure' skills and experiences that the area offers, and which skills and experiences are 'facilitative'.

You need to identify the pure and facilitative skills for each area on an individual basis. The general rule of thumb is that if you can do it in another area of the environment then it is not a pure skill specific to that area. If we were considering the water tray and were looking at the skill of pouring, this would not be a pure skill of the water tray as it can be done in other areas

The pure skills and experiences are usually the most basic ones, and many of these need to be experienced and mastered first by children. This is why the prime areas of learning and development are full of activities and resources to underpin pure skills. It is only when children have a good knowledge of the pure skills and experiences that they can apply that knowledge to other learning. Two of the main areas of stagnation in many Early Years setting are the sand and the water. More often than not, children will enjoy playing in those areas, but they will resort to very low-level skills and experiences because they can, they are familiar and they are easy. The prime areas of the EYFS are full of pure type skills, the specific areas are full of facilitative skills – that is why the skills in the prime areas need to be nurtured in the earliest years, but also need to be offered until the end of the Foundation Stage.

It is important that you constantly re-evaluate your children's skill development when they are learning through play, otherwise there is a risk that they will revert to very low-level skills that do not challenge them or enhance their learning. However, there are some children, not just those with acknowledged learning difficulties who will need opportunities to experience and develop pure skills throughout the EYFS (and sometimes beyond).

This links back to the idea of asking yourself during sessions of continuous provision: 'Can I see engagement?' 'Can I see progress?' Once the children have left the carpet and gone into play, you look up from your activity and scan your class like a meerkat to check that everyone is doing something. No one is in the toilets firing tissue out of the hand drier, no one is trying to drown anyone else in the water tray, all is well – or is it? The fact is that everyone being engaged does not necessarily mean they are all learning.

If we have not identified the key skills in our areas of provision, we are more likely to provide low-level, familiar resources that just invite children to engage (albeit happily) in low-level tasks. What you are risking here is long-term learning stagnation, where children become accustomed to lack of challenge. This can encourage children to 'butterfly' and visit lots and lots of different areas and activities because they are bored with the provision that you have put out. It can also result in children demonstrating inappropriate behaviours or just heading for the door as soon as it is opened and spending their entire time whizzing around on a scooter!

So, how do we avoid this situation? Well, if you want to guarantee success and avoid stagnation in all areas of your environment, then you need to apply a multi-layered approach. If any of the layers are missing, progress is at risk. How many children do you see who just stand at the water tray and pour? Pouring is great fun, but it features at 16–26 months in the Early Years outcomes, so at its basic level, it is not the most taxing! If we take the good old sand tray as an example, what we need to do is to identify the pure skills and experiences that you can get from the sand tray, and then identify the teaching and learning opportunities for developing these skills into facilitative skills which the child can use and practise in lots of different areas of learning. By doing this we can ensure we are planning provision that actually meets the needs of our children.

When I am carrying out this exercise with a team of practitioners, I start by taking a large piece of flip-chart paper and writing the area/activity we are focusing on at the top (in this case 'wet sand'). Then I split the page into two halves for 'pure' and 'facilitative' skills. I then ask the team to fill in both columns. 'Digging' for example would go under the facilitative heading because you can dig in areas other than sand.

Warning: this activity may make your brain ache, but it is a good ache and it will really help you when it comes to planning for your environment and tracking progress.

An example:

Wet Sand	
Pure skills	**Facilitative skills**
• Exploring the unique properties of sand (wet and dry)	• **manipulative skills** – digging, filling the bucket, turning it over, making a sand castle • **language skills** – talking about sizes of the buckets and spades, taking part in small world imaginative play, vocabulary, retelling a story in sequence, talking about experiences of sand at the beach etc. • **mathematical skills** – matching large spade to large bucket, matching colours, counting, sorting, comparing, recognising and naming basic shapes, developing one-to-one correspondence • **social skills** – respond to instructions, sharing equipment and space • **thinking skills** – investigation, discussion and problem-solving, hiding and finding, representing familiar objects in 3D form *and many more!*

Lots of the facilitative skills you could include aren't there and so the list isn't finished, but what this hasn't helped us with is those essential pure skills. So, what is it that is unique to the sand tray? Well in its broadest terms there seems to be only one pure skill or experience and that is 'exploring the unique properties and texture of wet sand'. This is often referred to as 'the sandiness of sand' (*so* Early Years!).

However, children need to have lots and lots of experience of the unique properties of both dry and wet sand before they can apply what they know to other learning. Teams often try to add 'making a sandcastle' to the pure list. Although it is true that you can only make a sandcastle out of sand, what you make it out of isn't really the skill. It is how you make the castle that is important. When you make a sandcastle you are exploring the manipulative skill of 'moulding' – you are 'moulding with sand' – a facilitative skill that you could also develop in clay, dough, mud or pastry.

Lots of sand and water areas are full of very low-level resources that invite children to return to pure skills and experiences. If we are confident that our children are very secure with the pure skills in each area then we should be planning for facilitative skills and experiences. Identifying these will give you a much easier planning focus and more realistic continuous provision planning.

Levelling your skills and experiences

Once you have identified which facilitative skill and experience you are going to enhance in your provision, you need to level (differentiate) that skill according to the ability levels of your children. If you have got a broad range of abilities then you will need a range of resources. If you have a much narrower ability spread, then your resource provision might be more focused.

If we go back to the sandcastle as an example, then we have already identified that the skill that we are looking to develop is moulding. Let's choose that for our continuous provision enhancement for this week in the sand tray. The next step is to take the skill and break it down into levels of complexity – three levels are usually enough. Again, a big sheet of paper and some pens will help your discussions as you work through the skill development from basic through to advanced. Here is the sort of thing you might come up with.

Level One: children at an emergent skill level

> Q – If we think about the skill of moulding, what is the most basic way that children usually create a mould?
>
> A – They do it using a flat hand and they tend to drag and compact it into large heaps.

(Incidentally, any skill that involves the use of a flat hand is usually very basic. If printing was the skill that we were looking at, and we were trying to identify the most basic or emergent way that a child would make a print, it would be with the flat hand. So, be aware that any activity you plan where the focus is to get children to create a handprint is actually promoting a very basic level of development. If that is where your children are, fine, but how many dexterous Reception children are asked to create a butterfly hand print every year as an adult-focused activity?)

Level Two: children at a developing skill level

> Q – Once they have progressed from raking and compressing with their hands, how do children then create a mould?
>
> A – They will probably use some sort of container.
>
> Q – Can you describe what that container might look like? What characteristics make it easy to fill?
>
> A – It would have a wide surface area and be fairly shallow so that it is easy to turn over and turn out.
>
> Q – How do the children get the sand into the container? Can you list the items that they would use in order of skill and complexity?
>
> A – First they would use their hand, then perhaps another container, then a scoop because scoops are deep and have a short handle which makes them easier to

control. After scoop would probably come spade. The longer the handle, the harder the spade is to control therefore you would start with a short handle and make the handle longer for challenge. After spade you might use wooden spoons, again with different length handles, other sorts of large and small spoons and scoops.

Q – Once they can fill their shallow container, how do you make that more challenging?

A – Size and shape. A taller thinner container is harder to fill. A container with an irregular shape is more challenging. You could move from large irregular shapes to small irregular shapes like jelly moulds.

Level Three: children at an advanced skill level

Q – How can I make moulding even more challenging?

A – As well as encouraging the use of finger ends and pincer grip with smaller moulds, you can also significantly increase the size of the container and the filling tool. The larger scale and the increase in weight will present a whole new set of challenges around dexterity and control. You can even take it outside with full size buckets and spades.

Matching the levels to the children

Once you have identified the skill you are going to be focusing on and then broken that skill down into its levels of development, you can match those levels to the children you have. If you have no children at the emergent stage of development then you wouldn't put out the low-level resources in your sand provision. By the same token, if you have no children at the higher level of development, then you wouldn't put any of those resources out.

By introducing a skill focus into any area *and* making sure that all members of staff are aware of the progression of that skill, you can use that planning and knowledge to encourage and support children to include that skill in their work at an appropriate level.

Your continuous provision is now becoming directly linked to progress (through the levels) and attainment and focused on skills development. Children in this sort of provision are far less likely to stagnate. You would apply this thinking to your whole environment, making links between areas as often as you can. This is a big job, and best undertaken as a group, when you have plenty of time! When you begin to think in this way you will realise that almost every element of your Early Years environment can be levelled to provide opportunities for challenge for children. Everything from scissors to glue!

What do you mean, how do you level glue? Well, just apply the same principle.

Emergent, developing, advanced...What is the most simple gluing resource that we give children? – It's probably a glue stick. When children's experience and dexterity is developing beyond a glue stick, what comes next? Usually PVA with an applicator, and you can even level within this. What makes it easiest to apply? – a finger. Then what? – a brush. Then? – a plastic glue spreader or cotton bud. Why? Because each one requires more dexterity and is harder to manipulate. And after that? – Well it is not superglue – that could be disastrous! It is not about the strength of the glue, it is about the complexity of the skill.

Skills development

Everyone in your team needs to have an understanding of skill development in children, and how effective use of the indoor and outdoor environments can have a significant impact on children's progress and attainment.

Of course children's development both indoors and out is not purely linked to markers of academic progress and attainment, although the current educational climate puts us under immense pressure to work purely to these academic goals. One of the great joys about working in Early Years education is the opportunity to nurture children's imagination, language and ability to think creatively. As a practitioner you will be able to promote all these skills through the activities that you plan and the direct teaching opportunities that you create. But, we should also be ensuring that we are giving children lots of open-ended experiences in continuous provision that allow them to discover, experiment and explore within the environment around them both inside and out.

Regular assessment of children's life experience, language, talk and thinking skills should also be used to help you to enhance your provision with open-ended resources that will help your teaching to have impact on promoting and enhancing these essential skills.

Low-level skill – high-level objective

There are times when you are planning when you will actively plan for a challenge in continuous provision. We should all be on a constant quest is to ensure that quality learning is taking place for *all* children in our setting. This is hard to do in an EYFS environment, which, although packed with potential, is also packed with unlimited opportunities for children to stagnate in low-level activities that challenge no-one.

One way to be sure that individual children are engaged in their play is to do an engagement/progress tracking of individual children in your setting, and it has been suggested that Ofsted inspectors should incorporate this in their inspections of Early Years:

Case tracking

In **group provision** *the inspector must track a representative sample of children. As a minimum, the inspector must track two children. This number will increase where a provision has a wide age range of children, where children are in different rooms and/or where there are distinct groups of children. The inspector should identify children who have attended the provision for a reasonable period of time as this should mean that the provider has established the children's starting points and evaluated the progress they are making.*

(Conducting early years inspections; Ofsted; September 2014)

Tracking is a simple and straightforward process where you pick a child and track them when they go into continuous provision. Every five minutes, find them and write down exactly what they are doing, you may wish to also use the Leuven Scales (see page 13) as a way to check on engagement and wellbeing. After an hour or so have a look at your list and then try to identify any progress for that child in the activity they were taking part in. This will provide rich evidence about the engagement and progress of individuals, but is time consuming and best used to focus on children causing concern.

If you have an able articulate Reception child who goes into the sand and makes sand pies with a bucket and spade for ten minutes, you need to ask yourself these key questions:

- **Can I see engagement?** – You would hope that the answer to this question would be 'yes'. If the children are not engaged, it might indicate that there is an issue with your provision and the activities you have planned. Has this provision been linked to assessment, appropriately levelled and dressed for interest?

- **Can I see progress?** – Most importantly, can you attach progress to what you are seeing, or are the children just happily engaged in low-level activities and learning?

Obviously acknowledging progress can be a subjective thing. It relies on the observer having a good knowledge of the development of the children that they are looking at, and of the stages of development used within the EYFS Development Matters (Early Education, 2012) guidance.

You can also carry out a 'spot check', where you walk through your setting once the children are in continuous provision, looking at each area in turn rather than tracking a specific child. On this occasion you would look at all the children at play there and ask yourself the same two questions; Can I see engagement? Can I see progress?

Case study

I did an engagement/progress audit in a Reception class alongside a headteacher and we watched the play and learning in continuous provision with great interest. We were particularly interested in two boys playing outside, who had taken a bucket of water and a sponge each from the 'car wash' and were sitting on a wall talking to each other while squeezing the sponge in the bucket. This went on for some considerable time. Just two boys, squeezing a sponge! As instructed, the headteacher asked herself the first key question. . . 'Can I see engagement?' Well, the answer to that was a definite 'yes'. The boys were very engaged in their sponge squeezing! Then she asked the second key question 'Can I see progress?' and decided that the answer to that question was 'no'. The boys had been sitting in the same spot for close on 20 minutes talking and giggling and doing a very good impression of messing about!

The headteacher then talked to the Early Years coordinator and asked her if she had been correct in her judgment, and if so, why had no one had intervened and taken the play forward? The coordinator said that she too had spotted the 'sponge squeezers'. One was a child with English as an additional language and as a result was a very reluctant speaker who often played alone or with an adult. The fact that he was engaged in an interaction with another child (and enjoying it) was a significant step for him, therefore she had left them to their sponge squeezing!

This example shows why any observation or judgment should always have some context from the people who know the children best. If you do observe your children and a pattern of high-level engagement but low-level progress repeats itself a number of times for a number of children then you have got a problem on your hands, especially if the children are compliant. Some will be happy to sit in your snack area, mark making or constructing for 30 or 40 minutes getting on quietly, but producing something that they could have done this time last term or even last year.

This may be partly because children like to make self-affirming familiar choices, and partly because the provision has not been set up for skill development, so even if an adult did intervene and try to promote more effective learning the planning and resources are not in place to make that a very easy task. Once your initial point of entry assessment is done you will then be able to set up your environment based on what these assessments tell you. Then you can start the circle of observation, assessment, planning, adjusting what you plan to include the children's interests, and this will continue until these children leave you and the next lot come, when the whole process starts again!

Within an effective environment you will have areas of continuous provision that will provide children with lots of opportunities to think and explore *but* that also will be linked to next steps' development and then 'dressed' to children's interests. Even with all of this good stuff in place stagnation can still come calling on a fairly regular basis. Key areas of any setting where he is most likely to strike are sand, water, malleable materials, workshop and paint.

Of course all of your areas of provision should look like play and feel like play, and its easy to get obsessed with levelling everything and turning everything into 'adult-led activities from a distance'! Alongside your continuous provision and enhanced provision you must also have open-ended resources that allow children to think, explore and engage freely, without intentions, objectives or levels. Only you will know the secret of when and how to use the levelled skills activities to meet the needs of individuals and groups, and of course, you will share it will your entire team, senior management, local authority and Ofsted. They will be impressed!

Making it interesting

Labelling and dressing for interest

If you have levelled your provision based on the attainment of your children and have it all nicely set out on your shelves, your next and biggest challenge is to get the right children to access the right resources. Otherwise, what was the point? There is a common occurrence in all Early Years settings during continuous provision known as 'trash time'. It takes approximately 17 minutes in Nursery and about 25 minutes in Reception for all the lovely resources that you have levelled and neatly placed in your areas of provision to get taken out, used and left lying around. Often by the time you get to the end of a session there is literally 'stuff' everywhere and you have to put the tidy-up music on 'repeat' for at least 15 minutes to get the place looking reasonable again!

Picture this! You have a group of 'fine motor' girls who are into princesses and a group of more 'gross motor' boys who are into super heroes. The girls never get involved in gross motor activities, seldom go outside, and when they do, they just sit down and do more fine motor stuff, looking at the boys rushing all over the place and making a lot of noise. The boys rarely go indoors, except when they have to, and they never sit down out of choice, and rarely get involved in any fine motor activities. You spend Sunday creating two lovely boxes of resources, one that contains lots of things that challenge and develop fine motor skills (for your target boys) and another that challenge and develop gross motor skills (for your target girls). You put these two boxes in your mark-making area and hope that the target group of children might, perhaps, come in and pick up the correct resources, but . . . sadly, probably they won't!

However, what might happen if you 'dress' the fine motor resources and the box in a Ben 10 theme, and the gross motor box in a Disney princess theme? If I am one of your gross motor target boys, I am more likely to come into the mark-making area in the first place because I can see a Ben 10 box in there. When I get in there I am more likely to put my hand in the Ben 10 box than I am the princess one. Therefore I am significantly more likely to be accessing a resource that has been specifically chosen to help my development. You *cannot* guarantee that this will happen every time, but what you can do is say with confidence that you have maximised the potential for progress in continuous provision and minimised the risk of failure.

This method of 'dressing' can be very successful but can sometimes be a little bit too generic. It may be that you have a group of children who are all interested in dinosaurs, but who have widely different levels of attainment, so a box themed around one ability level wouldn't be as effective. But when anyone asks you if you can quantify progress outside your focused teaching, the job just got a whole lot easier and as a practitioner, you can be secure in the knowledge that your continuous provision is really continuing the provision for learning and isn't just a collection of nice resources.

Using children's photographs

Another way of targeting specific resources is to use the children's images. Small photographs stuck on to wooden pegs works well. If you have differentiated resources around a particular skill – joining for example – then you could peg the faces of the children who needed to access a particular range of resources around the basket or box that those resources are in. You can then move the pegs as the children become more proficient and reuse them in other areas. For more useful ways of using children's photos (see page 76).

The task of unpacking the skills embedded in each area of your provision is a big job, but it is an important one if the children are to continue to build on their current skills and abilities as they play and learn in continuous and enhanced provision. Of course, you would need to spend time over a significant period to identify and list all these skills, and teamwork, or even working with your neighbouring settings, might help you to do the job. Hard work, but worthwhile, as then you can convince yourself that you are planning appropriate activities based on a real skills audit.

7 Direct teaching

In this chapter you will find some thoughts on planning for, and organising, direct teaching. These thoughts include exploration of how the children can return smoothly to continuous provision from adult-directed tasks, and how adults can continue to offer support in a systematic way to targeted children during continuous provision. An innovative and interesting process, referred to as 'objective-led planning' is illustrated with a case study, and followed by a step-by-step guide to the process. Finally in this chapter, I'll discuss how to maintain challenge in continuous provision, and give some examples of the use of challenge cards.

Probably the way that has the most impact in getting children to access levelled resources is through us, the adults, in adult-led or adult-directed tasks. However, for any continuous provision to work well, some of the adults *have* to be in it for some of the time, working and playing alongside children. Continuous provision will not work if adults are static behind tables running a focused activity or hearing readers. So you might decide that you are going to have three sessions of direct teaching each day, and that these will be at the beginning or the end of a session as you don't want to compromise the children's opportunities for sustained shared thinking, exploration and deep-level learning with some support from adults.

Great. That is that sorted! The problem is what do you do when the children leave you after the direct teaching? Well you have a couple of options. Once you have finished the input then you will say 'Red group you stay with me and the rest of you... go and get busy!' Shame for the red group having to do more 'work' while everyone else gets to go and 'play'. Still I am sure that they will give you maximum engagement, after all who wouldn't rather count buttons as opposed to playing in the water?

Once red group have finished, you have the eternal dilemma of what

you do next. Most people opt for developing a common condition known as 'tambourine elbow'. This is common in Early Years practitioners and members of the Salvation Army. It occurs from excessive shaking of the tambourine! So, red group have finished and while their seats are still warm you reach for the tambourine and shake it. Everything (well, nearly everything) stops. All the creativity, all the sustained shared thinking, problem solving, deep-level learning, imaginative play, everything! You then proceed with the 'I am looking for blue group' mantra and depending on the genetic make-up of blue group, this could take some time.

After five minutes you have managed to corral four of the six children, but two are still AWOL. They are outside on the bikes or making guns. Telling them that if they don't come in *now* they will never go out again, probably does nothing for their levels of engagement – but at least you have managed to rally the blue group, safe in the knowledge that in approximately 15 minutes the tambourine will come out again and the herding of green group will begin! I try to give one solution to this dilemma in the section below.

Teaching in a staggered return to continuous provision

The teaching style described here is particularly suited to Reception groups. If you work with younger children, you would need to adapt it, for instance to have the outdoor area available at all times during continuous provision.

I have talked a great deal in the continuous provision section of this book (see page 36) about how practitioners can unintentionally encourage poor attainment by withdrawing groups from continuous provision. Not only is the adult 'stuck' in one place with one group of children, but there is no one in the continuous provision to ensure that it remains continuous and doesn't degenerate into low-level, non-challenging, basic play.

There is also a real danger that children who are called away from a continuous provision activity when they are fully engaged will resent being disturbed, will not engage

fully with the adult-led activity you are calling them to, and will probably not return to the play activity when you have finished with them, probably ending up aimlessly flitting from place to place. So, if you are not going to withdraw groups of children, when do the children get the opportunity for more focused intervention and recording? The sort of mark making that you might get as part of a role-play situation is often very different in quality and content from the sort you might get if everyone was sitting around a table with an adult.

One answer is to engineer a staggered return to continuous provision. How does this work? If there are two adults in your setting and one adult is leading a direct teach on writing, the other adult can be supporting progress and understanding of the children in the continuous provision. When the children who are at an earlier stage of development have had an appropriate level of input they can begin (or return to) the session of continuous provision with an adult present to provide support, encourage engagement and even help children to return to a previous activity if this is appropriate. One of the real benefits of this is that this second adult can protect an incomplete activity, such as a construction, a half-finished painting, or a small world arrangement until the child can return and decide whether they want to complete it.

Because in Reception classes there is usually only one adult in continuous provision, then you probably wouldn't open up the outdoor space for reasons of supervision. The more able group who have stayed with the first adult can now go on for some further input or recording, and when they have finished, along with their adult, they can join the continuous provision. Once all adults and children are back in continuous provision, then all children can have access to all areas, including outdoors.

If you have younger children, and therefore probably more adults, you can group the children for their direct inputs and run the same system as above. As each group finishes their input and appropriate follow up, they join the rest of the children in continuous provision. As each adult returns with their group, they would then pick up their objective-led plan (see below) and join the children in play. In an ideal world you would take the children who would be focused for the longest period of time into a space where they wouldn't be disturbed by the other children returning to continuous provision. This could be in part of your space, outdoors or another part of your building. However, if you use a system of objective-led planning, where adults are delivering objectives to children consistently through their play, you will have more opportunities to focus their attention and your input on clearly levelled objectives.

Objective-led planning

Objective-led planning is the most effective way of taking teaching into children's play that I have ever used. With objective-led planning you still need to group the children by ability based on your observations and assessment. In this way, rather than having 'red group', 'blue group' and so on, it allows you to group your children more flexibly by their specific need in each area of learning. So, children who need more support in talk development and less in fine motor can get just that, rather than being in one ability group for both.

Once you have decided on your teaching focus, you group your children in relation to their attainment within that area. For each group of children you need to:

- **make a statement of their current performance** or 'where they are now' in that area

- plan a **next step** for each group – it is this next step that you then take into the children's play.

The success of objective-led planning is based on the fact that you go to them – I would *not* call groups of children to me. When you go and play alongside children you get much higher levels of engagement.

If you come across a group of children of mixed ability – which you will, because children don't tend to play in ability groups, you just differentiate your questioning to suit the next-steps objectives for the ability group of the child you are working with.

Example

If I know that I have got a group of children who have a particular interest in a specific superhero then I might create a 'starter activity' that I know is going to grab their interest, and station myself there.

Once children have visited my activity and I have fulfilled my teaching objective then I wouldn't start calling other children over. The activity has fulfilled its purpose in attracting the children that I was targeting. I would now take my objectives (not the activity!) into other children's play.

When the children are in continuous provision, the adults go into the play to look for opportunities for assessment and observation, to support children's play and discovery but also to teach, delivering an objective that has been identified by assessment as a need, linked to the EYFS guidance, and then been broken down into next steps for each ability group.

The objectives in each of these plans for adult intervention in continuous provision would 'probably' last for a week. I say 'probably' because children's learning is not an exact science and sometimes one objective will take much longer to cover than another. During that week the adult (or adults) responsible for that objective would try to deliver it to all the children at least once through play. They would probably *not* have a planned activity, like the example above, that they take around the setting. Instead they would look for opportunities to deliver the next-steps objectives through the resources and ideas that are engaging the children most at the moment. If a child you were working with didn't understand or achieve the objective then you could revisit it a number of times in a number of different areas across the week. By the same token if a child clearly showed that they were beyond the objective that you had set for them then you could revise that objective and offer it to them again in a different play situation.

I have found that any more than three objective-led planning sheets in any one setting at one time is hard to manage and track. In larger settings adults often double up on one objective and just present it in different ways.

Objective or activity driven?

Because this type of planning is based on delivering the objective to the children in play and *not* pulling the children out of play to come to an activity, most of the time you would not be planning an activity for everyone to do. For continuous provision to be really continuous, you have got to manage it, be mobile and become part of it. Having said that, there are times when you are using objective-led planning that you would have a 'starter' activity. This would be something that you know will really inspire lots of the children to want to get involved.

The important thing to remember is that you are using this as a springboard, something to get you started. When the interest in your starter activity begins to dwindle, you are not going to go out on the prowl, with your list of children who haven't done it yet, and drag them in! You would leave your activity and go into the provision with your objectives, looking for opportunities to deliver your next steps there. Regardless of how good you are or how exciting your activity seems to you, there will be children who are far more motivated by doing other things. You need to seek out **their** area of motivation and capitalise on it.

Objective-led planning with or without a starter activity? A case study

This example of objective-led planning shows how you could begin to incorporate it in your setting. In the case study, one Early Years setting trialled working on objective-led planning with and without a starter activity. This was partly to see what difference it made, but also because one member of staff felt more confident with a clear starting point, rather than heading off into continuous provision armed with nothing more than a clipboard. If you are very used to being given an activity planner and a group of children to work with, then this can be a very scary prospect.

This is what happened.

The teacher

In this EYFS setting there is a teacher and a teaching assistant. The teacher has a writing focus for her objective-led planning. She is going to encourage the children to write using their knowledge of phonics. She has identified and 'grouped' all the children according to their phonic knowledge and given each group a 'next steps' statement. This grouping is not a physical 'red group come over here' grouping, but a grouping that helps the teacher as she moves among the children. As she does this, she knows which 'next step' has been identified for each child – at the early stages, it's very helpful to have these groups written on your clipboard.

The teacher has *not* planned an activity. She moves from area to area, observing children, supporting their learning and as she does so, delivering her objectives. She finds opportunities for mark making and writing in all areas.

The teaching assistant (TA)

The TA has a mathematics focus for her objective-led planning. She is working on simple addition. She wants the children to count groups of objects and then combine their total. She *has* planned a 'starter' activity, and linked it to the interests of a group of children who are often difficult to engage in focused activities. Her theme for this activity is 'Pirates'. She has based it in the outdoor sand tray (for a bit of extra engagement), and she has buried some coins in the sand for the children to find, hopefully counting them and adding them together as they do. For added effect she has donned a pirate hat, a patch and a broad Cornish accent, that is coming out more Welsh/Irish!

She introduces her activity with great flair, and there is a lot of interest, not only from the target group, but also lots of other children. The children are working in mixed-ability groups and the TA is able to use her objective-led planning sheet to differentiate teaching and questioning as she works. Initially she tries writing any extra notes on yellow 'sticky notes' but they get very sandy, stop sticking to the clipboard and keep falling off, so she resorts to writing on the back of her sheet! Once interest in her activity has dwindled, she has a go at taking the objective into other areas of play. She delivers her objective during this session in the areas for malleable materials, small world, construction, workshop, mark making and snack.

Both adults felt that they were able to deliver their objectives successfully. As they discussed the session, the teacher said that because the TA was stationed at the sand table for a long period of the session, she had less time to focus on her own objectives, as she was having to spend time 'maintaining the environment' – otherwise known as tidying up behind the children, sorting out disputes and answering requests! Overall though, they felt the session had gone really well, and the TA said that she was now feeling more confident to have a go at doing a session without a starter activity.

Maintaining the learning environment

As I mentioned in chapter 6, at several points in every session, Early Years settings experience a phenomenon called 'Trash Time'. No matter how well you have coached the children in the use of an area or how expertly you have labelled your resources, there comes a point when you look up from what you are doing to find that literally within the last two minutes the environment has gone from organised learning opportunity to a scene from *Stig of the Dump*.

This just happens because children are actively using the environment and, with the best will in the world, they are not going to always wash their paint brushes after they have used them or put the scissors back into the right pot.

When Trash Time happens, it has a significant effect on the potential for progress in your continuous provision. You have used assessment to plan your areas, you have stocked them with appropriate resources, you have 'dressed' some of those resources for interest and you have even enhanced two or three areas with a skills focus. You have indeed dressed your environment for learning success! But, unless children are supported and helped to choose the right resources, and unless the right scissors go back into the Spider-Man tin and not the Princess tin, then your well laid plans are likely to fail.

One of the many benefits of objective-led planning is that Trash Time is less likely to be a problem. Because the adults are mobile during continuous provision sessions, and they are not stuck at one particular table or even one particular area, they are constantly moving through the space looking for opportunities to support children's learning, observe and assess them and deliver their objective. While they are on the move the adults should also re-set any of the areas they visit. I am not talking about a full scale tidy up, just literally a one minute re-set which they can either do on their own or with the children. If every adult did this as a matter of course during continuous provision, not only would the environment remain more effective for teaching and learning, it would also take the children far less time to tidy up, which in turn would give you more learning time, and have the added benefit of lowering your stress levels.

How to get going

Although objective-led planning promotes high-level attainment by capitalising on children's high-level engagement, it can be a huge shift in practice for some practitioners. My advice is to start small and work together. For a first attempt at objective-led planning, follow the simple guidance set out above, and repeated here for clarity.

Work as a team to:

- decide on your teaching objective
- make a statement of each child's current performance or 'where they are now' in that area, so you can group the children
- discuss next steps and work out a next step for each group – it is this next step that you will take into the children's play, and give every member of the team a copy of
- give everyone their own copy of the objective-led planning sheet with all the groups on it

- decide who will find and work with each group
- during a session of continuous provision, go to the children and have a go all together
- compare notes on what happened.

If your colleagues are less confident, don't give everyone individual objectives until they are confident with working on one group objective together.

Just one last thing that it is worth mentioning to your team... objective-led planning is a method of teaching that enhances and supports children's play. It is not a list of children that you have to 'get through' at all costs! Sometimes you will see opportunities to listen, support and engage that are nothing to do with your objective. You just pick it up and put it down as the opportunities present themselves. If you approach a group of children in play and they give you that 'back off with your clipboard' look, then back off. The beauty of objective-led planning is you can always 'get them' next time!

Ensuring challenge in continuous provision

Providing challenge in continuous provision can be a tricky old thing. It is hard to get that balance between 'encouraging' children to take on a challenge while still maintaining a high level of engagement, and 'telling' them they have to do something and risking low levels of engagement and low levels of attainment.

There are two main types of challenge in continuous provision – implicit and explicit.

Implicit challenge

This is what underpins how your environment is structured and resourced. Your environment should be linked directly to summative assessment, and the areas of provision that you put in it should be levelled to reflect children's current ability in that area. Implicit challenge also comes from a large dollop of ambiguity by offering lots of open-ended resources and experiences that encourage children to explore, investigate, think, ask and answer. When it comes to challenge, ambiguity is always your friend!

Explicit challenge

This usually comes through request or even direction. It can be very informal, where adults in the setting will prompt or ask children to carry out a particular task, or construct a specific challenge on an ad hoc basis, depending on who they are working with. Or it can be more formal and apply to all children.

Two settings have been experimenting with explicit challenge in continuous provision through the use of a challenge book or challenge passport. Both are still at the 'tweaking' stage, but are experiencing very positive responses from the children and positive results in engagement, wellbeing and progress.

Example 1

One school has introduced a challenge card for both their Nursery and Reception children. The children have been split into groups. Each group has its own symbol. Each child has their own card, which shows their group's symbol and their name. The idea is that new challenge sheets can be inserted inside the challenge card every week, keeping a record of the challenges that the children have completed across the year. Staff choose the areas that would have a challenge in them based on assessment, observation and need. There is *not* a challenge in every area (that would be completely unmanageable). There is also a space for any member of staff to create additional challenges.

In the areas chosen for challenge the team created a talking postcard on which they write the challenge and also record it. Children know which is their challenge because it has their group's symbol on it. During sessions of continuous provision, children can choose to take their challenge card into play, find their challenges and complete them. When they have completed a challenge an adult 'signs it off' and/or gives them a sticker for their book.

Points worth considering...

- As the children are in 'broad' groupings for all subjects it means that differentiation between learning areas isn't possible on the challenge card, so the adult would need to take on the role of recording this.

- If you put all the challenges in all the learning areas on Monday morning, it is a lot of work, and some children will just motor through them all to the exclusion of everything else. It might be worth considering putting a challenge in three learning areas on Monday, three on Wednesday and so on. This way you stagger your week and your workload.

- Challenge cards for very young children have risks attached! Take care that they don't dominate or take over from free play.

Example 2

Practitioners at the second school are also having a go at using a challenge card in Reception and Nursery. In Nursery, the children are grouped by key person, so at this stage their challenges are very general. This is to get the children used to the idea and the system. Each key group in Nursery has a 'mascot'. It is these mascots that the Nursery teacher has linked to specific challenges. The challenges are written and recorded on talking tins.

This school has grown to a two-form entry in Reception for the first time this year. They are running their continuous provision sessions together so they are devising a challenge system that will work with up to 60 children over two classroom spaces.

Sarah, the teacher has given the children three different sets of challenge each, one for literacy, one for mathematics and one for more general challenges. The children have separate books for each literacy and mathematics challenges. Like the first school, the challenges are linked to the symbol on the front of their book. They are also written in the appropriate area and recorded onto a talking tin (or similar). The challenges are differentiated according to ability, so one group has to fill the bottle with the correct number of peas – all numbers are below five. The most able group, on the other hand, are using numbers beyond ten.

For more general challenges Sarah doesn't use a book, she uses a mini me system (a photo card, with space for stickers, which is easily accessible on the challenge area wall). Each week the type of challenge in that area changes and staff just move each mini me around to create differentiated groups depending on what the new challenge is, and children complete the challenge below their own mini me. When they have completed their challenge, their mini me gets a sticker! It is very easy to see who isn't visiting the challenge areas.

Once again, on my visit, the children were very enthusiastic about getting their challenge books out and completing their challenges. There was lots of evidence of adults asking the children to do a 'bit extra' if they achieved their challenge too easily. If a child completes all of their challenges, they get an extra 'star slip' which is part of the school's reward system.

Although this system was working extremely well and it was making challenge in continuous provision very visible, my only concern was around the amount of preparation that Sarah and the team were putting in on a weekly basis. The outside of each child's book is laminated and folded with holes punched for treasury tags. Each child gets a weekly insert sheet with a new set of challenges on it. The challenges that go into the areas are be differentiated by colour. (They could have been differentiated by images, but this is much more fiddly to produce.) So in a challenge book, next to mathematics, a child might have a red dot or sticker. Next to mark making, they might have a purple dot or sticker. As they go into each area each child looks for their colour, making differentiation a much less time-consuming task.

Explicit challenge should always remain *firmly fixed* in the ethos of good Early Years practice. It should be activity based, dressed around children's interests and *fun*. If it is dull then children will not do it. Their challenge books should be a choice, not a requirement. If children don't want to do them it says more about the type of challenge you have set up than it does about the child!

Adult-led activity is the most sensitive element of the practitioner's job. Get it right and it's magical for both adults and children, but if you get it wrong, nobody learns anything! A commitment to following the children's needs really works as it takes the adults to the children and enhances their play by focusing on identified next steps.

8 Effective use of display

This chapter is about one of my favourite parts of the job! I have always been a creative practitioner, but I am aware that creative adults can very easily take over and crush the children's creativity in a need to express their own creativity! I have described some of my own early experience as a teacher, but only as a cautionary tale! In the rest of the chapter I try to focus very much on enabling children to express themselves and on raising their self esteem as we display their work with care and respect.

What is display for?

The definition of the word display is to:

> Put (something) in a prominent place in order that it may readily be seen.
>
> Oxford Dictionary

I think where we can sometimes go wrong with display is being clear about what the 'something' is that we are displaying and why we are displaying it in the first place.

When I first started teaching, display was something that you tended to do en masse to make your space look attractive. It was done exclusively by adults, and opinions of your ability as a practitioner related directly to how good your displays were. Mine were bright and I mean *really really* bright, we are talking foil wrapping paper for a backing, a tinsel boarder and fairy lights! It was all going on – clashing backing and borders, things hanging down, things popping up. A bit like a bad migraine really!

I was a teenager in the 80s. My most impressionable and formative years were soaked in bold colours and high-level accessorising. I had some zebra stripe baseball boots that I wore (with pride) with bright blue trousers, a canary yellow shirt, orange tie and an emerald green cardigan, and I was, or so I thought, the very height of 1980's teen fashion. My world was full of vibrant block colours, zips, fringes, diamante brooches, badges and of course fingerless gloves. When I became a teacher, I think I just transferred my inner teen from the 80s on to the walls of my classroom. The brighter and more clashing I could get it the better.

My thinking at the time was that if it was bright and vibrant that children (and adults) would like it. Displays were always linked to the topic. I would plan them in advance and then I would give children activities to create a display, regardless of assessment or links to learning. I once did the entire Nativity scene by drawing around children and then getting them to fill in the spaces using scrunched up balls of tissue paper. It took weeks!

Rather than display the work that children were creating, I found that I seemed to spend a lot of time giving them work to create a display. 'This afternoon we will all be sponge printing with green paint on these large leaf shapes that I have cut out.' This style of display stood me in good stead for many years until I began to consider the purpose of classroom display and what impact the display was actually having on the children and their learning. I began to ask myself the question, 'Why exactly are we doing that? What are the children learning from it? Which assessment did I use to identify a need for that activity? Or, am I just doing this because I need a border for my jungle display?' How much of it was about them and how much was actually about me?

After many years of experience and observation, I have come to the conclusion that the purpose of display must be to motivate, celebrate or teach, and preferably all three! To do so, the children need to be at the centre of the creation of the display and it is their work that needs to shine out from our walls and boards. However, the truth is that even though my early teaching experience was a good 20 years ago now, I still see lots of elements of that sort of practice in settings today.

Think 'skill' rather than 'activity'

I remember my first 'in the style of. . .' experience. It was in a large primary school in Manchester. I was teaching Reception, and the planning called for us to 'paint in the style of van Gogh', using 'The Sunflowers' as a reference.

I loved it! The finished display took us about a week to create. I decided that we weren't going to do a van Gogh copy each, we were going to create a giant-sized version of the picture that would fill the huge display board next to my blackboard! (That tells you how long ago it was. We didn't even have a computer in the classroom let alone an ICT suite!).

During lunchtime I set up the classroom for 'painting'. I mixed all of the paints, matching them to the colours on my poster. I then added flour (for thickness) and PVA glue for the 'sheen' of oil paint. I grouped the children on tables (sitting down) and each group had one of the flower heads to reproduce. When I say reproduce, I don't mean interpret, I mean reproduce (almost to the brush stroke). I spent my time moving between the tables, enthusing, encouraging and 'adjusting' the work that children had produced, 'enhancing' their artistry with a tweak here and an addition there. Until, finally it was done.

The reason I remember this display so well is that other adults in the school loved it. It got me high levels of praise all round and even the junior staff were sent down to look at it (I know, even the juniors!). It got me so much kudos that I had a flash of inspiration, an idea that really showed off my inventive and creative streak. I would do the display again for the other side of my blackboard, only this time I wouldn't do sunflowers, I would do moonflowers. I think I made some tenuous link in my planning to hot and cold colours and before you could say 'death by disengagement' we were off! Because the sunflowers had been so well received, the pressure was on to make this one just as good. As a result the children got even less freedom than they had the first time round. One heavily directed week later, there it was, and here it is. . .

I was so thrilled with what I had done that I took photos and kept them! Everyone in the school was so thrilled that I was asked by the headteacher if I would take it down and put it up again in the entrance hall, so everyone who visited the school would see it. I had arrived!

This is an example of how I think display has lost its way. Surely everything we do with children is about expanding their knowledge, skills and experiences. We are encouraging them to be creative and unique, not to be carbon copies of someone else. Also, our walls are part of our learning space and should be there to support and celebrate teaching and learning and not just look pretty. The main issue with effective display is adults (like me) who celebrate the coordination, colour and 'prettiness' of what is on the walls and don't question the skill, learning and engagement that went into creating it.

Display doesn't have to be dull, but it should be meaningful, relevant and full of learning. I am not saying no one should ever look at van Gogh's sunflowers in the classroom ever again, but rather than everyone paint a sunflower, teach the children a skill using van Gogh as an inspiration. If they don't paint a sunflower, does it matter? I would say the answer is No! absolutely not.

Example

Now, don't get me wrong. I like van Gogh. If you are going to 'do' a painter he has something for everyone. Don't forget, there are some children who will visibly wilt at the sight of a vase full of yellow flowers. If you are thinking about trying to get high levels of engagement then flowers don't always do it! But, van Gogh came up trumps due to the fact that he was a little unhinged and chopped off his own ear (now that is more like it)! Better than that, he then painted a picture of himself in a rather fetching bandage. . .

When we look at the 'style' of an artist that is exactly what we should be teaching. What techniques did van Gogh use that made lots of his pictures have the same feel even though the content and colours were often different? In essence for me, it comes down to 'very thick paint' and using something other than a brush – fingers, a play dough tool, a kitchen spatula. I am sure van Gogh didn't use a kitchen spatula but the whole point is that we don't want children to paint exactly like van Gogh; we are looking at style. Like everything else in EYFS it should be about teaching children a *process* that they don't associate with one thing but can creatively apply to many situations.

You should *not* get all the children to produce a version of 'sunflowers' because the learning outcome was not 'to accurately produce a copy of a great masterpiece', but to explore some or all of these objectives from the curriculum guidance for Exploring Media and Materials:

- *Explores what happens when they mix colours.*
- *Experiments to create different textures.*
- *Understands that different media can be combined to create new effects.*

By saying to children that they must all produce a version of van Gogh's painting, you are setting them up to fail and closing down any chance of them expressing their own creativity. You need to identify the 'technique', and the 'process' and then let the children experiment with it, producing any sort of picture they want to. You do not give children work so you can create a display, you display the work that they create using the processes you have taught them.

So... if you have sunflowers in your setting and you look at their sheer gorgeousness you might well talk to the children about this bloke who is famous for painting pictures (and cutting off his ear). I would:

Show them *his painting of sunflowers and a variety of his other work.*

Tell them *that he used oil paints, which are thick and shiny.*

Enthuse *over how fantastically squidgy thick shiny paint feels, especially when you apply it with your fingers!*

Then **show the children how** *to mix really thick paints by adding flour to ready-mix paint to really thicken it up and some PVA to make it shiny when it has dried (just like oil paint).*

Then just let them go for it! *Your display will not be 30 versions of van Gogh sunflowers but paintings using thick paint inspired by the work of van Gogh.*

Of course once you have opened children's minds to the possibilities of thick paint you need to make sure they can make their own whenever they are inspired to do so. When we teach children a new skill we then want them to be able to apply it to a variety of situations and not think that you can only use thick paint if you are painting sunflowers with a bandage over your ear!

Good Early Years teaching should always focus on what the children are learning from the 'process' rather than just planning for the outcome and as your display is part of your learning environment, a good display can reflect skill differentiation and attainment as well. One thing display shouldn't be is wallpaper. It needs to be meaningful to children and it plays an important part in the learning process. To make display meaningful to children, they have to be involved in its creation or appreciate the relevance of it. That is why, for the beginning of the year (if your year has a beginning) I would suggest that your walls are blank. They can be backed and bordered, but otherwise empty. True blank canvasses for the children to fill.

I appreciate for some people the thought of doing this would be a huge leap of faith, but trust me, it is worth it in the long run. If you have display already up when the children come in to your setting they will all notice it, but only a small number will really see it and of that small number very few, if any, will go on seeing it and then using it to support their learning. It just becomes very familiar and because they were not part of creating it and it isn't relevant to their learning, they just don't engage with it. I have never worked with a setting yet where the children have come in and seen empty display boards and then called for 'more colour' or 'more display' before they can begin their learning!

I have, however, come across a number of adults who really struggle with the 'emptiness' and feel that it is a poor reflection on their practice or their setting. The truth is that within a very short space of time your boards are going to be overflowing with quality display linked to learning. I would rather wait and have that than a mass-produced alphabet poster that no one looks at. So, if we are going to strip all our boards and back them in preparation for our new cohort, what should these boards look like? As I have said, in my day, I was the king of the contrasting backing and border, and there was no combination too bold for me to try. But, do you know what? I loved it, my headteacher loved it and parents loved it. They loved it because it was bright (very bright) and cheerful and busy. In fact, all the things children like. Only, this was a learning environment that was supposed to support, not distract children on their learning journey. Being children, they didn't have the same experience, visual perception or misconceptions that the adults had. It is not the displays that make an inspiring or outstanding teacher. It is their ethos and understanding about child development, which is why those displays eventually had to go.

Display is there to help, inspire and promote children's learning. So, what is on that display needs to be relevant, purposeful and accessible to the children. They need to engage with it, understand it and then use it in their everyday learning. Even though when they first walk into your space after you have been 'creative' with a display, they will 'ooh' and 'ahhh' at the fact it has changed and that it is bright and colourful, they will soon stop looking at it because it isn't relevant. Another problem is 'over-mounting'. If a child has produced a brilliant piece of mark making and you have backed it in pink and orange and stuck it on a gold foil board with a glitter border they will cease to see it because it will be lost amongst the brightness and the bling.

A sense of the children

In an Early Years environment that has really good display, I should be able to stand in the middle of the room without having spoken to an adult or a child, or looked at a planning file or observation, I should get a *strong* sense of the children who occupy the space. I should be able to see evidence of their voices having an impact on their environment. I should be able to see how their personal preferences shape the learning, and how their self-esteem is raised by seeing photos of *their* achievements everywhere.

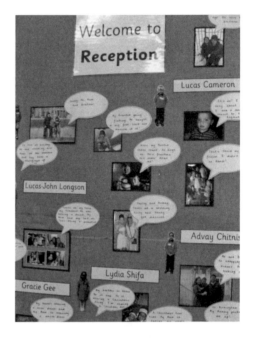

If I stand in the middle of a space and face a wall full of computer generated, downloaded laminates (however pretty they look to adults) I could be in anyone's space, anywhere. It may be bright and the walls may be festooned – but for children it is dull and lacks any sense of motivation or impact.

Children need to be able to identify their own work within a display. This visual stimulus will remind their brain of what it was they were doing when they created that piece of work, it will also remind them how happy you were when they had finished it and how proud they were when you put it on the wall. This will then inspire them to apply their knowledge or skill that they used to other tasks that they do. Hence your display is having a direct impact on attainment.

But first the children need to be able to see their work. It should leap out as the most important thing on that board. Make it easy for young, developing brains to be able to discriminate within what they are seeing. For that to happen the background of your boards needs to be neutral, I would go as far as to say beige, but that doesn't mean beige and boring! There is a real difference between neutralising your background so the children's work stands out, and neutralising everything. The advice to make your backgrounds calm and distraction-free means that the children's work and your teaching display can 'pop' out as a real focus. I have seen brilliant displays that have used a completely monochrome approach. It had a fantastic level of impact as well as being really clear, celebratory and informative. The assessment focus that had generated the images for the display was around children's grip and fine and gross motor movement.

Early Years should be an exciting place to play and learn and display should be a reflection of that. But the energy and 'wow factor' should come from the content not the dressing.

If you do decide to go for a more neutral background, there are lots of simple things that you can do to stop your displays from becoming insipid and dull. Here are some ideas using various other natural materials to pick out accent colours or create interesting borders:

- Don't be afraid of a bit of 3D. Tactile resources such as fir cones, small fabric samples, corrugated card etc. can really lift a display and give it some interest.

- Hessian makes a great background especially if you use a more ornate frame. A collection of different frames (without glass) can have a permanent home on the wall. Staff can then just change the pictures that go behind them.

- If you haven't got a stock of gilt frames (and who has?) you could always use pasta frames. Unless you could find a really good and convincing learning objective to attach to a mass frame making activity, the frames would be made by adults, and used for impact on specially interesting pieces of work.

Gender in the environment

One point that is worth considering when you have finished any display is whether you have made any statements that are 'gender specific'. Some boys' aversion to all things pink is not a conscious thought process, but a well ingrained learned response to gender roles that has been passed on to them. Usually these are well established by the time a child is about two.

So, when you are thinking about your display, make sure that your backgrounds are neutral but also that they do not cater too much for the preferences of one particular group of children. The game that I like to play with settings is 'If you had to give "it" a gender, what gender would you give it?' The 'it' can be any aspect of your environment or provision, but in this case we are talking about display. If the answer to your question is clearly 'male' or 'female' then your dressing is not neutral enough. This should never be the case unless you have specifically dressed an area or a resource around the interests of a particular group of children.

Gender is *not* the same as sex. The World Health Organisation says that:

*Gender is the **characteristics**, **roles** and **responsibilities** of women and men, boys and girls, which are **socially constructed**. Gender is related to how we are perceived and expected to think and act as women and men because of the way society is organised, not because of our biological differences. (www.euro.who.int)*

So, it is possible to give the spaces that we create a gender whilst not necessarily intending them to be for 'boys' or for 'girls'.

One of the issues that often arises in Early Years spaces is that because they are predominantly created by people with a strong female gender imprint they can then appear very feminine to children who have a more stereotypically masculine view of gender. Gender stereotyping is a complex and subtle thing and most children have got a very strong gender imprint by the time they come into the Foundation Stage.

The socially accepted view of the gender that has been attached to their biological state will have been thrust upon them from the moment they were born, from the colour of the babygrow we put them in, to the type of language and cultural references that we use about and to them. When we are thinking about the environments and displays we create and how they appear to all children, then all that gender stereotyping and conformity comes into play. Not all of the time with every child, but most of the time with most children.

So, once you have sorted out how your displays might look, you then need to work out what you are going to put on them.

Print-rich or just full of print?

'Print-rich' is a lovely phrase, but it is one that is easily misinterpreted and can cause practitioners a great deal of angst not to mention headaches for children! So, what is a print-rich environment? Well, for me the most important word in the phrase is not 'print' it is 'rich'. If we think about the word rich in monetary terms, it just means that you have got a lot of it. But when it comes to learning through print, less is often more – at least to start with.

Print in your environment is only 'rich' for children if they are interested in it and engage with it. If there is lots of it then it just fades into the background. At the early stages of development, when children are recognising different letter and number shapes, print doesn't only need to be engaging, it needs to be clear. To an 'emerging eye' the letters a,o,b,d,c,p,q,e,g can look very similar, so if they are displayed all in the same font and colour within a very busy background then the chances are they won't be as engaging.

If we use print in the environment to teach children that 'print carries meaning', then it makes

sense for children to be involved in the creation of that print. This could include labels for the classroom or for displays. Recording what the children say about their work as part of the display, or what they think about what they have been doing alongside their photograph, can be a great way of getting them to engage with the print on the walls. I would also say that we should be offering children a variety of styles of print mixed with adults' and children's mark making, and writing that has been done 'live' in the setting. However, it is important not to confuse children with too much variety.

The main body of print on your walls should be meaningful and relevant to the children and produced by adults and children working together in the space. Enhancements to your printed environment can be made using other examples and styles of print. But you should view this sort of print in the same way as you do an enhancement to any part of your provision as just that, an enhancement.

Purposeful print

What is the purpose of a downloaded laminated display in your water area for non-reading Early Years children? Is it a well-known fact that children don't know how to play with water unless there are a few blue circles next to them with text they can't read? Even if they can read it – is it ever going to influence their play? It can be a really good idea to have labels near to provision to help, support and focus children's learning, but only if children actually engage with the print. A good idea is to help the children themselves to make the labels. Then you can talk about ideas and expectations while you are making them and the children will have a memory prompt every time they look at them.

If in doubt, do the squint test. Stand about six feet away from your board and squint at it. If the children's work, the background, the border and the labelling all merge into one riot of colour and pattern, then you might have got it wrong. If the children's work 'pings' out at you (and them) then you have got it right. After all, what is display for? It is there to motivate children by raising their self-esteem or to teach them something that they need to know. It is not about making wallpaper. There will be lots and lots of other opportunities for you to introduce print into your environment through books, comics, letters and so on. Just make sure your walls are print-rich and not just full of print.

Display to teach and inspire

We don't often think about a display being able to teach, but really, that should be one of its primary functions. To teach successfully, you need to engage, and that can be where some displays fall down.

To engage, you have to be visible, to grab the attention. I am not going to interact with something that I can't see or access. So, the ideal height for your teaching display is child-eye level, because human beings look ahead and down most of the time. This is how nature made us, so that we could scan the horizon for predators and prey and also look for food, resources (and big holes that we might fall into and die) on the ground. We had very few predators from above and few resources and food sources, therefore we don't really look up unless prompted to do so.

The further up the wall your display is, the less impact it will have for children without direction to it. This also applies when we are hanging copious amounts of 'stuff' from the ceiling, on hula hoops, washing lines and bits of string! Ask yourself the question, who looks at it? Also, what impact does it have on teaching and learning, and how does it impact in cluttering my space?

You have a water tray indoors. Above your water tray you have a lovely umbrella and from

that umbrella you have laboriously laminated and cut out lots of raindrops on which are printed adjectives that relate to water. It has taken you ages to hang them by thread from the edges of your brolly and you get really annoyed when the door to outside is open and they all blow about and tangle with each other! The question is the same as always 'Who is this display for?' Is it for children? How many children ever approached a water tray and said 'Now, before we start engaging in water play, let's just cast our eyes in a heavenly direction and reflect on some of these appropriately placed adjectives that link to water play'? The answer is none – *ever*! Does it really make it a print-rich space, when the drops are all the same size and same colour and printed in the same font and twirling round in the breeze? No! So, what is it for? Even though I have created many versions of this sort of display in my time for 'children', the answer is that this sort of display is for adults, because we like it, it looks coordinated and attractive and we can make the link between adjectives and learning. But children just don't.

As adults our brains are really good at taking in a lot of information and being able to sort it and process it quickly and efficiently. The majority of children have not developed that skill to such a high level when they are in Early Years. So, when they walk into a busy space, they don't see it in the same way that we do. Their visual discrimination isn't as well honed as ours, so everything tends to just blur into the background.

It is similar to when you say to a child: 'This is an a–pple a lovely shiny red a-pple! Listen to the sounds carefully. A-a-a-a- apple! Now then Connor, what sound can you hear at the beginning of **a**-pple? (bearing in mind that I have told you the answer!)?' Connor will of course answer 'c' as it is the only sound he knows. Not because it is the only sound he can hear, but he has been told that his name starts with 'c' and because his name is important to him, he remembers this. Connor is not deaf, he is just at the early stages of developing phonological awareness. He can't yet discriminate the initial sounds in words – but he will.

It is the same with visual perception, children see it all but they don't *see* any of it. It becomes background – wallpaper. So, the less clutter around the central display space, the more impact what is actually there will have – if they can see it. I know that most Early Years settings have not been built with this concept in mind. Often children's eye level is full of cupboards, sinks, trunking, units and so on, which is not ideal, but you can only work with what you have got and sometimes you have to get a bit creative with positioning your furniture and using the backs of units for display. One setting covered the backs of their units with ply board and painted it with blackboard paint, giving them a whole new range of child-height working and display surfaces. I know this will sound like a joke, but seriously, it is worth getting down on to your knees and 'walking' your space. It will give you a really good child's-eye view of what you have got to work with. It can be equally productive to do your outdoor space as well, but get some knee pads or kneel on a skateboard and get someone else to push you round – now that is how you could put the fun back into team meetings!

Once you have got your eye level sorted out, this is where you are going to put your key teaching displays, including things like phonic lines, alphabet charts, number lines and all the things that you want the children to engage with and use. The next step is to ask yourself 'What are young children motivated by more than anything else?' 'More than Spider-Man?' 'More than chocolate?' – *themselves*! They are ego mad. They love nothing better than to see themselves in a video or a photo. So if we are trying to create a display that will really motivate and engage them in their learning – a display that they want to interact with and return to, what should we use in that display? You've got it – *them*!

There are all sorts of ways that you can use children's images in display, and bearing in mind that you have just stripped all your walls, we had better get started at exploring some possibilities. I see lots of children's creations stuck up on walls. Once the child has completed their work of art, some adult has gone through the routine of 'Oooh, that really is fantastic! Now then, do you want to take that home (where it will probably be stuck a) in a pile, b) on the fridge or c) in the recycling?)

'Or do you want me to put it on our *amazing* 'Wall of Pride' where everyone in the whole world will be able to see how *spectacular* you are? – The 'Wall of Pride'? Are you sure? I wouldn't want to be seen to be influencing your decision. . . yes? Brilliant!'

So up it goes, with the child's name duly printed, laminated and stuck next to it which is great – apart from the fact that if I am four years old I might well be able to recognise *my* name, but I can't read so I don't know anyone else's and they don't know mine. However, if you stick my photograph up alongside my name then everyone knows it's me and I also get the self-esteem of seeing my face up on the wall. What I usually try to do is have about half a dozen laminated photographs of each child's face and when they have done something that you or they want to put up on the wall (or wherever) I dispatch them off to get one of their photos which goes up first before their name. One setting has the photographs stuck on to pegs with the child's name underneath. This made storage and access easy. When the child's work went up the peg was just clipped on to it wherever there was a suitable gap. It worked really well.

Another very successful photographic initiative is the personalised alphabet and number line. What self-respecting EYFS setting doesn't have a number line and alphabet frieze? It is part of the essential kit! The question really is, how many of the key children who you need to target ever independently look at said alphabet frieze or number line?

As adults, we are like children in a sweet shop when it comes to these classroom essentials. There are *so* many to choose from. When I began my career you could only buy them from the Early Learning Centre and everyone had the same ones. Now, with the advent of the computer download there are literally hundreds of options. The key is to remember who we are buying them for, and the answer is – not you! They are going to be a key component that we will use every day in our work to teach children the basic skills of literacy and mathematics. There will be some children who pick up these skills relatively quickly and easily with or without the use of the alphabet frieze and number line but there will be others who struggle, who have a little longer to travel down their path of development. So, when it comes to considering who we are targeting with this sort of classroom display, the answer is *them* – the hard to reach brigade.

The answer to this dilemma? Personalise your alphabet and number lines with children's photos. More importantly, personalise key teaching displays to the children you are targeting with that knowledge – *not* the ones who already know it. My name is Alistair and if my first teacher had wanted to create a personalised alphabet, then where better to start than with me? I was the child who she really needed to engage! I would have loved it and my classmates would have been far more interested because it was not some animated apple but me! (Preferably sticking my tongue out for the photo as this will make the children laugh and raise the level of engagement even further!)

Make the photos nice and big. If you get to a letter of the alphabet and there is no one in your class or group whose name starts with that sound then ask the children what *they* would like to put in the picture, and photograph that. Remember if it's an alphabet line that you are using to teach initial sounds then you can't have 'Charlotte' for 'C' or 'George' for 'G'. It has to be the sound not the name. These children will come into their own later on when you start doing blends and words starting with a 'soft g'!

With your number line, use assessment to identify who knows what in terms of number recognition. Then create your line by targeting the children who don't know for the photos, and make your most difficult to engage number 1! Trust me, it works wonders.

Early Years settings are vibrant and full of colour, and the adults spend huge amounts of time mounting, decorating and titivating the work that children produce. This work, often done in practitioners' own time, can easily become wallpaper or, even worse, some sort of competition within the setting. I have fallen into this trap in the past, and would encourage all practitioners to think again, moving to a style of display that has the children, not the practitioners at the centre.

9 Effective use of role play to enhance children's interests

The spiritual development of pupils is shown by their:

- *ability to be reflective about their own beliefs, religious or otherwise, that inform their perspective on life and their interest in and respect for different people's faiths, feelings and values*

- *sense of enjoyment and fascination in learning about themselves, others and the world around them*

- *use of imagination and creativity in their learning*

- *willingness to reflect on their experiences.*

(The School Inspection Handbook; Ofsted; 2015)

In this chapter, I will hope to enthuse you all to follow children's interests and creativity by enhancing role play and looking creatively at the potential of topics and themes in capturing children's interest and supporting their learning.

As a classroom teacher I was a great lover of 'the topic box', and used it to enhance children's passion for creativity – painting, making, music and role play – play about 'trying on' being somebody else. At the beginning of every school year, I thought – 'Great! It's Autumn and time to get the topic box out!' It seemed that all areas of the National Curriculum nestled within it just waiting to be released by doing the same activity that I did this time last year (and probably the year before!). I showed great diligence in the creation of my 'topic map' and was chuffed at the fact that I managed to shoehorn all aspects of the teaching that I needed to do into one topic title – however tenuous the link.

That was just it. My teaching was not based on the interests of children or really on the requirements of the subjects that I was teaching. It was driven by the need to fit into the topic. The topic was king! I am talking about 20 years ago now and you would think that things would have moved on since then, but from what I see through my work in schools and other settings, things are very much the same in many settings.

A diverse approach

High-level attainment comes from high-level engagement. To get maximum engagement for all children we need to have a diverse approach to the topics and themes that we use in our teaching rather than just stick to one. Assessment will tell you what the children need to know, and the hardest part is capturing their interest so that they engage in the learning process, when the knowledge has more chance of sticking!

It is imperative that you are really clear that when you are planning for effective learning, that you theme your teaching around children's interests, not the curriculum guidance and not their gender. Regardless of their gender you are going to 'dress' your teaching for children around what motivates them most. If the interest is dinosaurs, then you provide dinosaur activities. If it is princesses then you provide princess activities. This is nothing to do with 'boys' and 'girls', it is to do with interest.

Be prepared for children to interpret the stimulus that you provide in very different ways. For some children the huge egg that you leave outside for them to find may inspire an interest in dinosaurs, but others might think of unicorns or even giant chickens! (Who are we to say that unicorns don't hatch out of eggs, or that big eggs won't just hatch into bigger versions of birds we know.) Your planning and your teaching must be flexible enough to allow this to happen or you are saying to children that there is only one way that they can interpret their learning. . . *your way*!

The end product of the activities that you set up will not always lead to the same curriculum or previously defined outcome. The *process* of creating those outcomes is the important bit. What the children could produce can (and should) be applied to any theme that inspires them. You might create an activity to make dinosaur bread bones, but equally you could make unicorn horns, dragon's teeth or mermaid tails. It is the bread making that is the skill not the fact that you have made it into a bone. Most activities should offer children the opportunity to engage in a range of processes and create lots of possibilities for open-ended investigation and questioning. Our aim is always to get the children to master the skill or the process, not to get 30 versions of the same end result.

Some of your children might be highly engaged by the process of making fossils of dinosaurs out of dough or clay, but the process, and the skills needed, are all about using objects to make patterns and impressions in malleable materials, so if other children are more motivated by another subject or another material then that is fine because they can still be learning the same process or developing the same skill, just through a different theme. Of course, some of the activities and objects you provide are for inspiration or to engender some of that mystical stuff known as 'awe and wonder'. These are objects or experiences for *you* to create and leave for children to find or discover. Although you might have in your head what you think their response will be, be prepared to go with whatever they come up with, remembering that the children will probably not all think the same, and be prepared if necessary to go with more than one topic or theme at a time – a novel concept!

Plan for skill development, not end product. 'Dress' activities for interest and not gender. Teach objectives, but be prepared to dress those objectives differently for different interests and you will get some high-level engagement. Most of all enjoy the power, magic and individuality of children's imaginations and have some fun!

Role play

The truth is, it is not just humans who engage in role play as an important part of our learning and development, the animal kingdom is full of species who spend a great deal of their time playing to learn and learning to play. Play is crucial to our social development. It helps us to become familiar with our own preferences and feelings as well as learning to recognise the emotional state of others. A lack of role-play opportunities means that we do not get the chance to observe, practise and rehearse the subtleties of social signalling which make us effective and appropriate communicators.

Research has shown that active play stimulates the body to produce brain-derived neurotropic factor, which protects existing links in the brain and helps to produce new ones. It is particularly active in the areas linked to learning, memory and higher-order thinking. Basically, play is essential for sorting out how the world makes you and others feel and making decisions about what you need to do next.

Play is a safe ground for trying and testing out life without threatening children's physical or emotional wellbeing. Children feel safe because they know that they are playing. Even though children show a great capacity for being able to suspend their disbelief and become completely absorbed in the roles that they are playing, they still know that they are in play. Sometimes their actions step out of the realm of 'playing' (often in more physical 'superhero' play but that is also usually a conscious decision). For all humans, children and adults, what we play is what we know and what we have experienced. Sometimes our play will replicate real life, sometimes it is fantasy and often a mixture of both, as we try to make sense of the world.

In role play, children can imagine possibilities, think of possible outcomes to a specific scenario and then test their thoughts. It allows them to practise, imagine and rehearse problems and possibilities before they happen. Lots of

opportunity to do this will equip children with the solutions to most of the situations they will come up against, and the strategies for problem solving and a wealth of experience to draw upon. Role playing with other children not only reinforces social interactions but gives the children involved the opportunity to learn about the thoughts, reactions and strategies of others, which will in turn enhance their own.

Over-structuring and theming of role-play spaces can significantly get in the way of children developing these skills. It is difficult to expect children to be able to explore and make sense of their own personal experiences when they are being asked to do it in a Chinese restaurant or the Post Office! Although theming around children's interests can add value to a role-play experience, it should be an enhancement to your provision and not the provision in its entirety. If you want to give opportunities for 'thematic' role play, then baskets, bags and backpacks with grouped resources (or preferably collections made in response to children's requests) can help children to find a scenario that suits them. For a real quality role-play experience you need to provide lots of opportunities for social interaction and objects that will promote open-ended play. What is crucial is their imaginations can run wild and take a leap – if that is what they want to do. As children's knowledge of the world develops, imagination will take on a greater role in their play and they will begin to create simulated realities that they can explore without giving up their access to the real world.

Whatever you call it, 'rough', 'superhero' or 'weapon play' is a necessary part of children's play and development. It helps them to build and maintain appropriate social awareness, cooperation, fairness and altruism. It also ensures that they can distinguish between play fighting and real aggression. Role-play fighting is a common feature of development the world over both in every country and society. 'Play fighting' is also a feature of role play that is shared by the majority of the animal kingdom, particularly when they are young. Puppies, lion cubs, deer and many other animals play at fighting as part of growing up. Contrary to popular belief, such play in humans is not a precursor to violent behaviour, in fact there is an argument that if children were given more access to play fighting then the instances of 'real' fighting would be significantly less. Good role play interacts with and involves the outside world and imagination, but fundamentally it explores the individual needs and desires of the players.

Skills and abilities emerging through role play

Many of the skills and abilities we use in adult life have been learned through role play, and these are many and varied. Many experts hold the view that role play should be at the heart of education at all developmental stages from the Early Years to University!

Trying to understand what children are doing when they play in role is a complex activity. Here are some of these skills and strategies that children use as they play in role.

- Pretense – the skill of playing a part, being someone, something or somewhere else. In role play, children develop the capacity to use their imagination to feed their play.

- Storytelling – in every session of role play children tell stories – those they experience in real life, those they hear in books and those they make up for themselves.

- Using receptive and expressive language – children's skills and ability to listen to and understand what is being said to them and their ability to communicate their ideas and thoughts in a way that others can understand. Conversation and dialogue through verbal and non-verbal communication is at the heart of role play, even when a child is alone and talking to him/herself.

- Creating mental or imaginary representations – ideas, characters and themes that children create in their own minds and then play out through role play.

- Transforming objects – using one object to represent another. The more open-ended the object, the easier the process. So a box can be a boat, a house, a microwave, a shoe etc. Through this skill children can develop and use symbolic action – imagining how something 'might be' or 'might feel' – and then use this as a mechanism for their play.

- Negotiation and problem solving – using language and conversation skills to reach a compromise, solve a problem, or agree an end result.

- Choosing, selecting and deciding – children cooperate in play but decide on the role within that play that they would like to take, and how that character will behave.

- Directing others or being directed (the skill of cooperation) – children cooperate in play but are happy to be directed by another child or adult who is leading the scenario.

- Joint planning – children work together to come up with a plan, a story, a scenario.

- Flexibility and improvisation – children may originally have no set or fixed plan for how their play will develop. The scenario emerges as a result of the children's interactions.

- Expressing and demonstrating emotions – children explore and express a range of emotions in a safe and supported environment.

- Sensory motor skills – children make sense of the world through their senses and their physical actions.
- Abstract thinking – children think about the world around them in a different way and from a different perspective. For good abstract thinking, children need to be able to use and apply their prior knowledge uniquely.
- Understanding and obeying rules – children learn about explicit rules like playing fairly and sharing, and implicit rules such as collaborative suspension of disbelief, maintaining fantasy play, even though they know that it is not 'real'.
- Recalling and replaying their own experiences
- During role play children can also practise their social, interpersonal, physical, communication, mathematical, scientific and other skills in meaningful situations.

So, we want our role-play opportunities to encompass all of the skills above and more, but do they?

The risks and pleasures of themed role play

As a classroom teacher I was a great lover of themed role play. My role-play spaces would follow the same pattern, always prepared with a great deal of thought and effort (many weekends and holidays were lost to the creation of a cardboard café or spectacular pirate ship). Yet I often experienced frustration at not reaping the reward of what I wanted that role play to be. Children didn't bustle into my café, to be greeted by an enthusiastic waiter who would meet them, greet them and seat them with flourish, offering them the menu and reviewing the specials of the day. This was despite the fact that each and every table was resplendent in gingham and furnished with its own wipe-clean menu and fake flower in a vase!

Instead, they would rearrange the resources that had been set out. I would find menus on the floor and flowers and vases shoved into pots, pans, bags or cupboards. I seemed to spend my life constantly going into the area and berating the children for not doing it 'properly'! When I was in there doing my 'thing' their play was always very different and far more appropriate. It didn't occur to me for a long time that the reason for this was precisely because I was in there. I was structuring the play, giving a scaffold of experience that the children didn't have and very much leading (I would probably now say, dominating) their play and learning.

If you are looking at the work of the vet, or what happens at in the Post Office or exploring the culture of China (through a restaurant!) then add these as enhancements to your open-ended role-play provision. But, and it is a big but, be prepared for children to interpret the stimulus and enhancements that you provide in very different ways from the ones that are necessarily in your head.

If you provide a gorgeous box of Chinese restaurant resources and then some children decide to use the bowls to explore some domestic role play while being dogs, then that is alright. You wouldn't shout over 'Oi, put those bowls down, you can only use those when you are playing Chinese restaurant!' The

fact that the children are able to take something that you have introduced as a bowl for a Chinese restaurant and then reinterpret it as something else, shows a high level of imagination, creative thinking and transference. Role play in continuous provision should offer children the opportunity to engage in a range of processes and create lots of possibilities for them to develop key skills. Our aim is always to get the children to master the skill or the process not to get a replicated version of predetermined play.

More open-ended role-play provision will give increased opportunities for inspiration to engender some of that mystical stuff known as 'awe and wonder'. You can enhance the play space with a huge variety of objects or experiences for the children to find or discover. Because there is no 'theme' your enhancements can be random or linked to specific interests of groups or individuals.

Talk in role play

To help our children to become effective talkers we first have to make sure that we have created a learning environment that supports and enriches that talk development. It is true that talk at its most basic level is made up of thoughts turned into words that come out of your mouth, but there are a number of different types of talk that require different sorts of experiences and different vocabulary. Role play is a great way to encourage talk between children and, if adults join children in their play the language will be richer, and the adults can assess children's current levels of skill and where they need support, which can be provided in future role play or in other areas and activities.

Providing a talk-rich environment

A 'talk-rich' environment is one where children's levels of talk and vocabulary are accurately assessed and opportunities are created for further development and enhancement both indoors and out. Although talk is everywhere in an Early Years setting, it is good to identify the areas that lend themselves to particular types of talk development. For example, where in your setting are there most opportunities to develop talk for helping *'children to listen to instructions and be attentive'*? Where are there most opportunities for developing talk for *'extending children's vocabulary and teach them to use new words'*?

Knowing the different types of talk that you would like to develop will help you to create and resource areas that will support the children with their learning.

Children also need different sorts of spaces to develop different types of talk, from tiny private den-like spaces to great big open outdoor spaces. They should have spaces to whisper, spaces to shout, spaces to talk to one significant other, spaces to chat with friends and spaces to address a larger group. Many of these key spaces can be provided as part of thematic, interest-based role play. When you are thinking about areas to encourage talk you may not want to (or have the space) to create big areas that use lots of floor space. If that is the case then you can create lots of small areas in different parts of your learning environment both indoors and out.

In every space you will want to provide lots of interesting open-ended resources that will appeal to different children in different ways and inspire them to want to talk. You can also provide specific resources that are aimed at developing a specific element of talk. For example, when you are looking at developing the language of turn-taking then you would provide activities and games that need children to be able to acquire and use that language before they can take part.

Opportunities for children's talk

If the children you are working with have little or no language for the type of talk you are trying to develop, then the adult plays a key role in modelling and supporting the introduction and use of that type of talk. Once the children start to become familiar with using the talk then they need lots of opportunities for practise, and role play is an ideal place for this to happen. When it comes to types of talk, such as talk for conflict resolution, this will come up as part of children's everyday play and interaction when something has gone wrong or someone has taken an extra turn on the bike. As adults we often get caught up in the drama of the situation and provide a 'quick fix' resolution to the problem. What we don't

do (often because of time) is discuss options and possibilities for an effective resolution in a way that a child might be able to comprehend and understand.

To be able to compromise, children have to first be able to feel some empathy for the person that they are going to have to compromise with. So if conflict resolution is an issue, don't wade straight in with high tension conflict activities that will more than likely end up with one of the children giving the other a push, punch or slap (because they don't have the language or skills to communicate efficiently)! Start by creating talk activities that are based around empathy. If possible take the 'personal' element out of it so that you are not re-enacting a real event that has already happened involving the children that you are working with. This will only serve to raise their stress levels and remind them of how angry they were.

Role-play situations

Think about how you could create role play or small-world situations where children can translate their thoughts and feelings through other characters. In this way they do not feel inhibited, embarrassed or judged and are more likely to be receptive to the play. I have found it really powerful to introduce a miniature version of the children themselves into their small-world play. A 'mini me' system (see page 68) is very simple to make and provides unique opportunities for talk development.

Children will often use fantasy, small-world and role-play situations to practise and rehearse their talk, either revisiting actual experiences and replaying them through role play or creating an imaginary situation and talking their way through it. The size of your role-play area and the resources that you have in it are of paramount importance. There is no point saying that you want to develop children's talk and then having a tiny role-play area that only three children can fit into!

Space for role play, whether this is full body 'dressing up' or the use of small world, puppets, characters from TV and DVD, or just space for the talk that involves 'being someone else' won't be wasted, especially if the play is routinely joined by adults who may:

- **play in parallel** by starting an alternative story using a different character and sitting near the group with a hat or cape, a puppet, small-world figure, or their own mini me – waiting to be invited to join the story
- **ask** if they may join the play in progress, having first watched and waited until they understand how they could join without taking over
- **model** new role-play situations with other adults, as a group of children watch
- **bring** new resources to enhance the existing theme of the play
- **use role-play areas and resources for adult-led activities** – home corner stuff is very useful for maths activities!

The key to effective role play for language development is the ambiguity, flexibility and open-endedness of the core resources that are in it. If we over-theme our role-play space then we are stifling children's ability to consolidate and enhance their vocabulary and use of language. To role play anything, you have to have had experience of what you are going to role play – otherwise how do you know what you are supposed to do? It is worth remembering that a cardboard box is never just a cardboard box when it is being played with by a child with even just a little bit of imagination. A post box, however, is a post box unless it being played with by a child with a very vivid imagination.

Keep your 'core' role-play resources simple and unthemed. Include cardboard boxes, tubes, crates, fabric and den-making materials. Enhance this with 'real' objects that you have collected to support a theme or interest. Once you have set up an open-ended provision for role play in your setting then you need to be strategic in how you are using that provision to meet the specific talk needs of your children and develop their skills.

Role-play talk skills

To develop a successful talk skills provision, you should plan the specific skills that you are going to focus on across a given period of time and then resource the play to support that skill development. So, instead of planning to create a Post Office, which everyone will have to play in whether the Post Office is relevant or interesting or not, you plan to develop a talk skill that can be applied wherever the children's imaginations take their play. Here is an example of the sort of skills you would be thinking about:

- talk for social interaction– build relationships, cooperation, take turns, join in, share
- talk for making choices and decisions, developing curiosity
- talk for developing language – using familiar and newly introduced vocabulary
- talk for developing communication and negotiation skills
- talk for expressing emotions and feelings
- talk for recalling own experiences
- talk for developing mathematical language and concepts in a meaningful context
- talk for develop day-to-day activities like cooking
- talk for communicating ideas in construction of props
- talk for projecting themselves into feelings or actions of others e.g. fantasy characters from TV, fairy and folk tales
- talk for taking on a role in an imaginary situation both real and fantasy
- talk for conflict resolution, both real and imaginary
- talk for problem solving in real and imaginary situations

Even:

- tidying up! – talk for negotiation, organisation

This list is taken from; *Get Them Talking, Get The Writing*; Alistair Bryce Clegg; Featherstone Education; 2012

Small-world play

Providing flexible and open-ended resources to develop dramatic play is not just confined to your role play. Plain wooden bricks in your small world can have the same effect, only in miniature. A toy pig is always a pig and a toy car is always a car, but a small plain wooden brick can be a hundred different things depending on whose hand it is in.

Just as play indoors and play outdoors can be very different, the same thing applies to talk. We need to make sure that our small-world play is not just resigned to the carpet area or the farm but that we give opportunities for children to play with their small-world resources outdoors in 'real' environments full of 'real' objects that will not only provide a setting for their play but will also support them in the development of their language for the real things that they can see, hear, smell and touch. In the same way that you would plan for a skill development in role play, you would do the same for your small world.

Small-world play talk skills

Here are some examples of some of the talk skills that you might plan to support through small-world play, and of course, many of these will overlap with the role-play talk skills above:

- talk for size comparison and properties of small-world resources
- talk for cooperation and collaboration, begining to work as part of a group
- talk for sharing and turn taking with the small-world resources
- talk for the exploration of role play with small-world characters
- talk for naming of familiar objects and animals
- talk for the development of descriptive language
- talk for positional language
- talk for naming attributes of common objects and animals

- talk for developing an awareness of a real-life environment that is different from their own
- talk for communicating emotions e.g. fear
- talk for discussion of previous experiences that were both good and bad
- talk for description and exploration of colour, texture, shape and size of objects found in 'real' and imaginary habitats
- talk for awareness of danger
- talk for recognition of 'sameness' and 'difference'
- talk for finding out about past events in their own lives and the lives of others
- talk for making choices
- talk for organising ideas and experiences
- talk for expressing feelings and ideas.

Of course, quality talk development is not restricted to the role play and the small world. There are opportunities for talk development in every area, it is just that some lend themselves to the enhancement of particular types of talk more than others. Wherever you are in your setting and whoever you are with, don't underestimate the power of quality talk.

Topics and themes are particularly powerful if they expand throughout your setting, and particularly in role play. Many practitioners are now committed to following children's interests and 'fascinations' by providing extensions, resources and equipment, including clothing and artefacts that inspire the play and take it further. This way of working is less predictable, and often involves supporting more than one topic at a time, so it can become complex and demanding of resources and adult time. However, this flexibility is good for everyone, and often results in surprising outcomes that affect all areas of learning and can involve some of the less committed children in your group in making real progress and demonstrating surprising skills.

10 Effective ways to inspire children: Thrill, will and skill

In effective settings, practitioners will:
Choose unusual or interesting materials and resources that inspire exploration.
(Development Matters; Exploring and using media and materials;
Early Education; 2012)

We need to consider that without thrill there is no will to take part and without the will, how will children successfully acquire the skill? Turning the thrill of learning and the will to learn 'by doing' into skills and aptitudes for learning, both indoors and outside.

Inspiring children is a major part of a practitioner's job, and when children are inspired to learn they are far less likely to be difficult to manage, as behaviour always improves when children are engaged in learning. In this section, I will explore how looking at the thrills of your setting, and managing these to capture the will to learn, makes life more manageable, enjoyable and productive.

Why children behave as they do

The unique child:

- *Shows understanding and cooperates with some boundaries and routines.*
- *Can inhibit own actions/behaviours, e.g. stop themselves from doing something they shouldn't do.*
- *Begins to accept the needs of others and can take turns and share resources, sometimes with support from others.*
- *Can usually tolerate delay when needs are not immediately met, and understands wishes may not always be met.*
- *Can usually adapt behaviour to different events, social situations and changes in routine.*
- *Is aware of the boundaries set, and of behavioural expectations in the setting.*

The adult could:

- *Name and talk about a wide range of feelings and make it clear that all feelings are understandable and acceptable, including feeling angry, but that not all behaviours are.*
(Development Matters; Exploring and using media and materials;
Early Education, 2012)

So, you have got these children (possibly, but not always, boys) who, every time the door is opened stampede towards the outdoor area and plant themselves on a wheeled toy. Then,

the fun really begins. . . crashing, banging, hurting, destroying, fighting. You know the score. First of all you ask nicely for more appropriate behaviour. Then you tell, nay demand, better bike etiquette. Then you threaten confiscation of the wheeled toys or compulsory eviction from the outdoor area until attitudes improve. The problem is. . . attitudes rarely do, or at least not on a long-term basis. The issue isn't really about the equipment or the behaviour itself, it is more about the reason *why* the children behave in the way that they do.

Some of the behaviour can be attributed to how children need to make sense of the complexities of their developing world and some of the behaviour is very much about the environments that we create and the provision that we put into these environments. I have worked with practitioners who resort to the 'lock away' method, which consists of locking away all the wheeled toys to 'teach children a lesson'. This is not a great solution for any number of reasons, but primarily because a lot of what the children are doing is perfectly natural and normal behaviour, and finding an equally satisfying alternative to crashing their scooter into a stack of milk crates is beyond their immediate control or will.

The thrill factor

Very few children in Early Years, who when their favourite thing in the world is confiscated and 'locked away' take time for a period of reflection, inwardly examine their misdemeanor and then vow to be better citizens! They just get grumpy and find mischief elsewhere. Part of the reason why lots of children behave inappropriately on the wheeled toys is simply because they can. They know how to ride a trike, they can ride a two-wheeler bike at home, so how can they make trike riding a more exciting and thrilling activity – go faster, much faster! Go on two wheels! Crash into other trikes or equipment! Shout and yell as you ride! Carry two of your friends on the back! Chase the other, quieter children! Ride round and round in circles till your get dizzy! You get the idea!

If we look at a group of children whizzing around a track at 50 miles an hour taking corners at 90 degrees, they are showing a very high level of skill and dexterity on the piece of equipment that they are using. In that respect, the resources are not providing challenge. The children find it easy to manipulate and that is why they like it. They crash into each other on the bike track, not because they have poor coordination and direction skills, but because it is fun, exciting and a little bit dangerous. It is this *thrill* that gives them the *will* to want to engage. What we need to do is capitalise on this and make sure that what is on offer also develops their *skill* level.

What you want them to do is too easy in terms of skill, so they ramp up the risk factor, which in turn increases the thrill. If you have children who are heading for the door, the simple fact is that there is nothing – I repeat *nothing* in the rest of your provision that they find as thrilling as being outside on the bikes. Usually there are no instructions, they just get on and do what thrills them until someone tells them to stop. Every area of provision that we create should be placed there in response to a need that we have identified through assessment and observation. Our provision is there to support and extend children's learning, and this could be social, it could be physical, it could be academic – it is there for a reason. But what about wheeled toys?

Power and control

The other reason that children can behave in this way is their very natural desire for power and control. Although we may give children a range of choices within their everyday routines, we rarely allow them full control of what they want to do and how they want to do it. Rightly so, this is because children have not yet gained the knowledge or experience that will equip them with a range of options, decisions or choices.

Through this type of 'crash and bang' play they get the opportunity, in a controlled, safe and supportive environment, to explore what is possible and what is dangerous and they experience cause and effect in relation to their actions. They can take 'safe' risks, which will ultimately help them to take more calculated risks in the real world. They can create and explore simulated realities without having to change what is happening in their own 'real world'.

So, there is a large element of physical role play (this also spans superhero and weapon play) that is a perfectly normal part of children's social and emotional development and should be expected and supported rather than locked away. But there is also a large part of this type of play that is done purely because of the thrill factor. For the solutions to this issue we don't need to look to child development but to our own provision. Why not give your setting a 'thrill test'? The thrill doesn't have to come from big physical activities. It comes from any activities with high levels of engagement. Thrill can be small and quiet as well as Ta-dah! The one essential thing that you need to be able to provide a high level of thrill within your space, is to know your children.

Undoubtedly, when you discover a dinosaur bone in your digging pit, if fairies have moved into your outdoor area, or an alien space ship has crash landed outside the window, these events will promote high levels of engagement because they are 'an event'. However, although this type of event is great fun and hugely valuable, and it would be very difficult (and impracticable) to have one of these every day. Imagine the following scenario. A bank of computers is three boys deep. You could certainly say that you were getting the thrill and the will but this is another situation where the skill is often lacking. If you really observe what the children are actually doing, are they developing social skills and turn taking? (Very unlikely.) Are they taking their learning forward with programs that will extend and challenge them? (Again, unlikely.) Are they engaged in low-level provision thinly camouflaged as learning? (Yes! Probably.)

What I am saying is that if you have gang mentality on your wheeled toys and scrums around your computers, and constant confrontations in your construction while your workshop area remains void of testosterone and full of sparkly pom-poms, then you need to have a rethink.

Thrill, will, skill audit

Take some time and do a thrill, will, skill audit of your setting. Identify your areas of thrill (easy) they will indicate high levels of will, but then do the harder bit. . . take a long hard look at the level of skill development that is taking place so you can adjust it accordingly. This is not only about the children (frequently boys) on wheeled toys, it is also about children (frequently girls) who will sit in mark-making or workshop areas for long periods of time and produce beautiful pieces of work that do not challenge them in the slightest. Regardless of their gender, find out what thrills your children and just make sure that you use that thrill to actively support the development of skill.

Are the wheeled toys you offer actually giving children any challenge? Look at the wheeled toys children have at home. They will probably have two-wheeled bikes, skateboards, go-carts, skates and other toys that provide a challenge that trikes, scooters and dolls' prams just don't. Of course, Reception aged children (and those in Years One and Two) have a right to outdoor play and wheeled toys, but just providing them with the same sort and size they had when they were three does nothing for their self-esteem, let alone their skills, and all they have left is to see how many dangerous games they can think of to play on them! We must all think creatively about what 'adventurous activities' and 'wheeled toys' means for older, more physically adept children, and what sort of activities will enable them to have the will and the thrill while developing appropriate skills.

Teaching through other areas of learning

One of the most successful ways to engage children, especially when you are thinking about the teaching of basic skills, which can be more than a little dull, is to teach through other areas of learning. If phonics sessions are always done sitting on the carpet looking at the board and mathematics is always done sitting in a circle with a whiteboard and pen in your hand, it is little wonder that lots of children disengage.

When you come to planning your basic skills teaching, that you will be delivering to the whole class or smaller groups of children, you need to actively plan to do it with a focus on another area of learning and development. Say, for example, that your focus was on numbers and counting and that it was the beginning of the school year, so you were also looking at signs of Autumn. You could get a good collection together of Autumn leaves, conkers, beech nuts, sycamore keys and so on and rather than counting multi-link, you could count and group your Autumn finds. In this way you would cover your mathematics objective, but through understanding the world. Or, you might decide to get the musical instruments out to teach addition and subtraction. Give each child an instrument, call it by its correct name, play it, explore it (let them get it out of their system). Then tell the children that they have one instrument each (which they all now know the correct name for and how to play) and you have got two instruments. What you are going to do is to play so many beats on one instrument and so many beats on the other and the children have to add them together and play you back the total. I appreciate that this is not like giving children free reign to play, explore and experiment with musical instruments, but to be able to do that all children need a point of reference, to know what a musical instrument is called and how to play it. (A tambour is not a weapon used for 'bonking' you friend on the head with!). What you have managed to do is to teach mathematics a bit more creatively, using music, rhythm, which not only gives the children a wider scope of experience, but will almost certainly result in a significantly higher level of engagement.

In a setting I visited recently, they were teaching phonics by putting letter beads into hair gel and letting the children pick them out with tweezers to make words. They were teaching their phonics through malleable materials, and helping with fine motor development on the way! Once the group had had their direct input, the activity was put out into continuous provision so that children could revisit it, or explore it if they hadn't

been in the target phonics group. In another setting they were using construction to build words and sentences before recording them – really simple, but really effective.

Which areas of learning and development you choose to dress your direct teaching in, can be dictated by particular interests of a group of children that you are trying to target. You can also use it as an opportunity

to introduce children to the exciting things that an area of learning has to offer. It could be that you have got some children who never visit certain areas of your provision because they don't associate that area with their own learning style or preference. By targeting that area through a direct teach you might just change their viewpoint. Some of what you 'dress' your learning in will be linked to what is going on in the world around us, like weather, seasons, festivals and celebrations, and some will be to target gaps that are showing up in your coverage. Whatever the reason, you just need to make sure that you have fun with it. Because, when you do – the children will.

You can also use teaching through other areas of learning and development to introduce skills to children. If you were looking at joining words together to make a sentence you could join your words using low-level, mid-level and high-level joins – the ones you have got as a skills focus in your creative area. One group might be joining their words with a paper clip, while another will be using a hole punch and treasury tags. You really can be as creative as you like!

Teaching in other areas of the environment

This is another great strategy for engagement, and also signposting learning opportunities around your environment that some children might miss because they don't visit certain areas very often.

If you are doing a direct teach and you are splitting your children into smaller groups, then where it is possible try to get each group to have their focus in a different area of the environment. By that, I don't just mean that they go and sit on a different carpet space and then get their whiteboards and pens out. Use the bricks for language by 'clocking' rhythms of words and sentences; use the paint to explore numbers and shapes; go into the mark-making area for a reading experience where children write words they know and hold them up for their friends to read; use the book corner to explore and compare illustration styles in favourite books or go outside with any activity, you'll be surprised how much more fun it is outside! If your group is too big or you are delivering a whole-class teach, then you can still teach in other areas of the environment, or think creatively about your teaching resources. You just have to bring the 'essence' of that environment to your carpet area. Try it – it is great fun!

Using the outdoor area

Of course you can take this principle to extremes – at a conference recently I was talking about what effective outdoor play might look like and one practitioner said that her school had recently been inspected and the Ofsted inspector had told her that she didn't have enough permanent alphabet friezes and number lines in her outdoor space. This prompted me to ask the question (which I often do). . . why would you have permanent alphabet friezes and number lines in your outdoor space?

It doesn't make any sense to me on a number of levels:

- Outdoor play is different from indoor play.
- Your outdoor play space *should* be different from your indoor space
- There is a *big* difference between outdoor play and indoor play that has been taken outside.
- No child ever stopped their game of superhero baddies and said 'I know we are having a brilliant game of chasing but let's just stop here for a moment and access this lovely number line and use it in our play!' It just doesn't happen.

When you have a teaching focus outdoors you might want to take counting/alphabet resources with you to enhance a play experience or deliver a focused teaching session but they don't make effective permanent features of your outdoor continuous provision. Apart from the fact that children don't access them, they get tatty, faded and generally unkempt very quickly. They don't enhance a natural environment, they are an eyesore! It is not just number lines and alphabet friezes, the same goes for all of the generic downloadable laminated labels that we stick up all over the place. Labelling your outdoor environment in this way does not make it print rich. The children don't engage with the print so it actually encourages them to ignore it.

The golden rule to outdoor play is that it is *not* the same as indoors, it should look and feel different and while you can build on some of the experiences that children have had indoors, it should offer them something different. A sand tray that has been pulled outside is *not* outdoor sand play. It is indoor sand play taken outside. Construction bricks on a blanket on the grass are not an outdoor construction experience but simply an indoor one taken outside.

Outdoors *has* to be planned as outdoors and *not* just indoors taken outside. I am not saying that I think indoor experiences should never be seen outside (on pain of death!). You might well be encouraging a child to pursue their particular interest with cars or construction, and support them in carrying this interest into the outdoor environment. Lots of children will enjoy mark making, reading and creating outdoors using resources from the indoor environment. I think we just need to be clear in our planning for learning in an outdoor space what experiences we are planning, who we are planning them for and why.

Outside play should offer children different experiences and the opportunities for different types of skill development. When the weather is warm and sunny lots of children choose to be outside. Therefore outdoor experiences are available, because that is where the children are. There are also some children in our cold and rainy climate who prefer to learn outdoors, and you might take indoor learning experiences outside for them, but your team needs to be aware that they are offering indoor skills and ensure that there are lots of other specific outdoor learning opportunities available.

I have worked with settings that have split their outdoor space up into areas of learning. There will be a mark-making area and a mathematics area, reading space, construction space and so on. It is just like an indoor learning space with the roof lifted off. Children who don't engage with these opportunities indoors are not going to suddenly start engaging with them outdoors. If I associate an alphabet line with phonics sessions that make my brain ache, I will apply that same association regardless of where the line happens to be hanging!

When children are working in their outdoor environment they are usually physically more active than they are indoors, both in the type of movements that they make and the range of movement. Outdoor play should offer the opportunity for children to initiate and take part in games involving personal interactions, conversations, negotiation and often conflict resolution. Society's attitude to outdoor play at home has significantly changed over the last 20 years. Children just don't go into the outdoor environment in the way they used to. The use of the car and parental anxiety, the advent of the computer and even 'garden pride' keep children indoors. This is all the more reason to give them access to an exciting and engaging outdoor space in your setting.

The outdoor environment should be filled with things that stimulate children's curiosity, things that are interesting to look at and investigate. A good outdoor space has pockets of ambiguity that are open to interpretation and exploration. The more 'themed' and structured your space is, then the fewer opportunities there are for children to really engage. And a bit of mud never goes amiss either!

Supporting learning

When you are working with younger children, the outdoor space really supports their emergent interests and schemas in a way that the indoors often can't. How many times have you set up an activity just to find that your inquisitive two year olds have picked half of your resources up and stashed them somewhere else for safe keeping? (Often down the toilet!) Outdoors has the potential to allow them to transport, fill and empty to their hearts' content without causing major disruption.

A well-planned outdoor space supports children in very tangible skills like gross and fine motor dexterity, coordination, physical awareness and control, and so on. It also develops children's concentration, creativity and ability to socially interact. Being active is also thought to have antidepressant effects. Physical exercise can be a mood enhancer for all children, but can have a real impact on children who present some behaviour management difficulties. Exercise is also really good for enhancing brain activity as it increases the intake of oxygen and the flow of blood to the brain. Studies have shown that children who exercise before academic testing improved their performance, so your outdoor engagement will have a definite impact on your indoor attainment!

When I watch children in outdoor play, they appear to feel less accountable than they do inside. Our expectations for the indoor environment are usually really clear whereas outdoors, although we will have expectations for behaviour, safety and so on, the lines are a little more blurred, the space is less predictable therefore there is greater freedom. It is in this sort of environment that children begin to take more risks and in turn feel more confident to embrace challenge. In a totally risk-free environment, you end up with risk-averse children.

Outdoor play benefits children in so many ways:

- emotionally
- socially
- physically
- aesthetically
- intellectually.

Sometimes it can be hard for adults to see outdoors as an environment for learning because it is so alien from what we perceive in education to be a 'normal' setting for teaching and learning. Outdoor play is not just recreational playtime, it is a fundamental part of children's development.

What should outdoor play look like?

So, if it doesn't look like indoors taken outside, then what might it look like? You want to make use of any 'space' that you have, however small, so it is a good idea not to fill it with large or fixed structures that will limit the potential for play and exploration and also the space for movement. If you are going to introduce any fixed structures, try to keep them open ended like a mud kitchen or a den space. If you start to introduce a permanent 'train' or 'pirate ship' then these outdoor items will only ever be a 'train' or a 'pirate ship' for most children. Rather than enhance and develop their outdoor play, the over-theming actually restricts it.

Lots of portable equipment like crates, boxes, tubes and guttering are ideal because you can move them about as well as offering great opportunities for children to use all of their communication, problem solving and collaborative thinking skills to build and create.

Try to keep your continuous provision outdoors open ended and ambiguous. You can then enhance that with resources that support children's interests, or ideas that you want to introduce to the children. Look for resources that encourage engagement, talk and play. Try revisiting the old traditional games like hopscotch and ring games. Spend time teaching the children how to play so that they can use them in their own games as well as alongside an adult.

Consider the power of 'superhero play', which is often perceived as being dark and dangerous. Actually, when encouraged and managed appropriately superhero play is the opposite and can be a very powerful teaching tool. As I have said, when we try to ban the making of weapons and guns, it makes them more attractive to some children because by outlawing them we have upped the level of 'thrill' in creating them. The fact of the matter is that they will do it anyway, but because they know they are not supposed to, the weapons they create are low-level and basic, easily hidden or deconstructed.

When we embrace their high level of engagement and provide support and resources to facilitate their interest the weapons that they create become infinitely more complex and show a significantly higher level of thinking and creativity. If we want our children to be self-motivated educators, then we have to give them an environment to interest, puzzle and inspire them.

Looking at the impact

- When you are considering the impact of your outdoors, stand back and watch what children (and adults) are doing in the spaces you have created. Are the resources that you have provided really outdoor resources, or are they just indoor stuff taken out?

- When the children are engaged in outdoor play, can you see challenge? Areas like the track are common for getting high levels of engagement but minimum levels of challenge and attainment. If your children really are whizzing round the track at 90 miles an hour on their three wheeled scooter then they are showing you that they have well and truly mastered that skill. If that is the case, then you need to capitalise on the engagement but add some challenge either by enhancing the track or changing the wheeled toys.

There is no one blueprint for a 'good' outdoor space, because each one will be different. But no matter if yours is huge or tiny, concrete or grass, the fundamentals are the same.

In lots of outdoor play experiences there will be elements of indoor resourcing. These often act as a familiar 'bridge' that allows children to initially access familiar equipment that will lead them into other types of skill development. Setting up good continuous provision outdoors can be tricky to start with, but you will make the job easier if you make sure to:

- Start with assessment to identify need.
- Reflect the need identified in the provision you offer.
- Link 'bridging skills' to indoor provision.
- Be clear and explicit about why you have put indoor provision outside (like your water tray).
- Be clear and explicit about how you are planning for the development of outdoor skills.
- Enhance your explicit outdoor provision with indoor provision (e.g. mark making, reading, mathematics) for added engagement and basic skill development.

Every area of learning and each part of your setting or school, indoors and outside, can offer places and resources to inspire children, and when there are problems with behaviour or even 'wilful damage' it may be time to do an audit of the way that area is engaging the children. Looking at the toys, games and equipment that children have at home, moving the equipment to another place, joining the activity yourself, or adding a challenge is often all you need to do to engage the children again. Regular audits of both your indoor and outdoor provision is an essential part of ensuring that the thrill, the will and the skill are all present and balanced.

11 Effective ways to organise your day

Effectiveness of the early years provision

A highly stimulating environment and exceptional organisation of the educational programmes reflects rich, varied and imaginative experiences that meet the needs of all children exceedingly well.

(The School Inspection Handbook; Ofsted; 2015)

Planning and organising the day is a constant concern for practitioners, and there are as many ways of organising an Early Years day as there are practitioners. Practitioners spend a lot of time searching for the 'Holy Grail' of the perfect planning format and process, sharing their plans reluctantly, but always very keen to look at other people's! We must be realistic – there is no 'Holy Grail'! The best format is the one that works for you! However you organise your day, as a conscientious professional, you will never have time for everything you (or the children) want to do. But be careful, sticking to a format because you have always done it that way can be just as dangerous as jumping onto the latest 'fad' or idea that you hear about at a conference. Flexibility is important, but constantly changing your plans and organisation will risk destroying children's confidence and undermining their wellbeing.

In this chapter I have tried to unpack the elements of planning and organising learning, illustrating these with examples from schools and settings. Read this chapter with caution, take the ideas and look carefully at your own planning before you decide to change it – if it works for you and the children in your care, don't change it!

Timetables

Although no two settings have exactly the same timetable, there are similarities that exist wherever I go. As I have previously said, there needs to be a good balance between adult-lead and child-initiated teaching and learning. In the current climate I tend to find that there is a very strong leaning towards adult-led delivery. This is because this style of teaching puts the adult very much in control and makes tracking input and evidence very easy, although it is not always the best model for learning.

Undoubtedly there has to be some direct teaching in Early Years, especially with regard to children's acquisition of the basic skills of literacy and numeracy. Having said that, there has to be a balance. As Early Years practitioners, we know what is appropriate for the stage of development of our children and should keep that firmly in mind if we are being asked to jump on to the latest literacy or numeracy bandwagon that will have our children sitting on the carpet 'chanting' for ridiculously long periods of time.

Assessment is the most important tool that we have at our disposal for letting us know what to teach and when to teach it. If children are not ready for a particular stage of learning then we should be using our resources to help to prepare them. If they are more than ready then we should take them to the next step on their learning journey. There is no such thing as the 'perfect timetable'. Timetables will change as the needs of the children change. Also in lots of larger settings you do not have the luxury of complete freedom with your timetables as there are so many other restrictions that are imposed upon you over which you have no control like assembly or ICT time. Everyone's timetable will be different and you have to do the best with what you have got.

After working with a number of settings over a number of years to support them in implementing objective-led planning within the restrictions of their timetable, this is the generic template that I have come up with. It should be 'tweaked' by your individual setting, but it might give you a starting point to get you going. Obviously, at the beginning of the year, or for a new intake it would be very different as children are getting used to you and your setting. Ultimately what we are aiming for is a timetable with a lot of fluidity and the minimum breaks. At the beginning of the year you undoubtedly have a timetable that reflects the opposite. You may be doing lots of stopping and starting to help children to be clear about how to use your space appropriately with lots of very public displays of delight when they achieve what you have asked.

At the point you are introducing this sort of timetable you will have already:

- Structured your environment around needs identified by your last summative assessment and ongoing observations, or the assessments of the previous practitioner.
- Levelled your continuous provision in each area, linked to assessment.
- 'Dressed' some of your continuous provision for interest.
- Created opportunities for exploration, problem solving and thinking.

Within this timetable there are going to be:

- Opportunities for direct teaching.
- Opportunities for teaching through continuous provision using objective-led planning.
- Opportunities to observe, assess and support children's learning.
- Time to talk to children and find out what interests and motivates them.

The timetable I have created follows below. It is split into two halves in the morning and in the afternoon.

In the morning

1. Self-registration

At the beginning of the session I am a huge fan of self-registration and have had great success with children from the age of two years and upwards being able to successfully self-register. This can be done in many ways:

- laminated photos 'Velcro-ed' or attached to a sticky strip
- name cards, lolly sticks or mini mes moved from one container to another
- charts of names or photos, and a felt pen
- a tablet computer or interactive whiteboard, where children can touch their photo or drag their photo or a named cartoon character into a virtual net, parking place, paddling pool etc.

The reason that I like self-registration so much is not just because it helps to develop children's independence and self-reliance, it also frees up adults to interact and support learning rather than go through the ineffective and over-rehearsed routines of days of the week and the weather. If I have just walked in from the outside, why would I want to sit and wait for the V.I.P to wander over to the window and assess the climate. Always remember that progress is directly linked to engagement. How much progress are children making during your morning carpet session?

2. Linked provision

This is a *short* session of 'linked provision' that takes place while the children are arriving and self-registering. If you work with younger children, you will know that they want and need to have access to the whole range of activities, although you may not offer completely free flow, indoors and outside. This session didn't exist in my first versions of this timetable but was introduced in response to a need identified mainly by Nursery and Reception teachers in schools. The provision here is not throughout the whole space but is usually just table top, or game/play-based. This gives you time to talk to individual children or parents and carers, picking up that essential information that will make your day go better.

Alternatively, the session could be linked to an area of learning and development identified by assessment. So, if you know that your children have a particular area of development that you need to focus on, such as problem solving, then this first session of continuous provision could be entirely linked to that. When this is the case, I would plan a weekly focus and have the same activities out every day for that week.

This session has also been used very successfully as a time to hear readers. Rather than pulling children out of learning through their longer continuous provision sessions, this session is used every day for an adult to hear individual or guided reading. The number of adults available and the length of the session will dictate the number of readers that you can hear. As the same provision is going to be available at this time all week then children are not as likely to 'miss a play opportunity' if they are asked to go and read.

Adult role

This session can only work if there is a minimum of two adults. One adult will welcome the children and facilitate the self-registration and access to the continuous provision. The other adult will be doing some direct input such as hearing readers, or speech and language intervention.

---

3. All together – interest session

This is a daily session where everyone comes together on the carpet to talk. During this session children will have the opportunity to discuss the things that are important to them and adults will be able to introduce new ideas and concepts to children, as well as signposting learning opportunities that are available that day. During this session you will identify and record children's interests, using that information later to shape your planning and provision.

I would always have one weekly 'talk focus' based on the type of talk children needed to develop, and that has been identified through assessment. I would record this talk focus on my weekly planning and also indicate any key vocabulary that I feel the children needed to develop in relation to it. This way you are showing how you are using assessment to identify need and then how you are planning to meet that need. Talk is a fantastic tool for Early Years practitioners and holds the key to unlock every aspect of learning. But talk isn't just about talking! There are many different types of talk and language identified in the Curriculum for the EYFS, and children should have lots of opportunity to experience and practise all of them.

In the revised EYFS, what was Communication, language and literacy has now been sub-sectioned into the Prime Areas of: Communication and language, covering: listening and attention, understanding and speaking, and the Specific Area of Literacy, which covers reading and writing.

If you use the age-related descriptors in Development Matters in the Early Years Foundation Stage (the non-statutory guidance to the EYFS) for Communication and language, they give you a very comprehensive reference point, not only for the type of talk activity that you should be planning, but also the national expectation for age-related attainment described in the Development statements for the Unique Child, and the Early Learning Goals, as described below. For example, the early statements for Speaking for children between 22 and 36 months include:

- *Use language as a powerful means of widening contacts, sharing feelings experiences and thoughts.*
- *Hold a conversation, jumping from topic to topic.*
- *Learn new words very rapidly and is able to use them in communicating.*
- *Use gestures, sometimes with limited talk, e.g. reaches toward toy, saying 'I have it'.*
- *Use a variety of questions (e.g. what, where, who).*
- *Use simple sentences (e.g.' Mummy gonna work').*
- *Beginning to use word endings (e.g. going, cats).*

And by the time they reach the end of Reception, they should be reaching the Early Learning Goal for Speaking:

Children express themselves effectively, showing awareness of listeners' needs. They use past, present and future forms accurately when talking about events that have happened or are to happen in the future. They develop their own narratives and explanations by connecting ideas or events.

The range of talk skills that children need and are able to develop is very diverse and complex, and this is far in advance of what they are expected to record in their writing, as described in the following Early Learning Goal for Writing:

Children use their phonic knowledge to write words in ways which match their spoken sounds. They also write some irregular common words. They write simple sentences which can be read by themselves and others. Some words are spelt correctly and others are phonetically plausible.

The statements in Development Matters provide a really useful reference for looking at what 'next steps' for talk might look like in your planning, but also for mapping your coverage of types of talk and use of language.

Of course, I wouldn't expect you to say 'right children, this week we are going to focus on talk for conflict resolution and here is some key vocabulary that I want you to use!' But if you have planned for a weekly talk focus and all the adults in the setting are aware of it and the key vocabulary, then you would take opportunities to support it as they arise. To support this daily interest session, I would have an 'interest board' where I could display ideas that the children have had or things that they have brought in from home that have promoted interaction and discussion. This sort of display also makes it really easy to track how children's interests are used in provision to promote high-level engagement.

Adult role

If there are two adults, then one will lead the 'all together' session while the other 're-sets' the environment after the first session of continuous provision. As this is not a taught session then it is a legitimate use of the other adult's time to set up the provision for the next session. They can join the discussion as soon as the set-up is complete.

---

4. Intervention to support physical development

Dough Gym and Funky Fingers session

Every day the children need to engage in some sort of intervention that is going to help them to develop their gross and fine motor skills as well as their sense of balance, coordination and proprioception *(the ability to sense stimuli arising within the body regarding position, motion, and equilibrium; even a blindfolded adult knows through proprioception if an arm is above their head or hanging by the side of their body)*.

As I have previously said, there is no point in just getting children to squash a few bits of dough in time to music if it's not going to have any impact on their fine-motor development. So the first port of call is assessment. You need to know where the children currently are in terms of their dexterity and then identify what the next steps are. To do this you need to take into account a child's grip with a variety of objects of different sizes and also their ability to use their own fingers, or manipulate apparatus or resources to pick up small objects. You can then use this information to create activities that will challenge and extend the children. During this session, the children who need more gross-motor development can then work with an adult on initiatives like Dough Gym. The following information is taken from my book *Getting Ready to Write;* Featherstone Education; 2013.

When it comes to Funky Fingers activities, the speed at which you ask the children to perform the activity, or the number of times you ask them to complete the task in a given time frame can really increase the level of challenge. Sometimes you will get a group of children whose dexterity is amazing, they could pick up a speck of dust with one eye closed! For these children I would organise some sort of activity that you can do to music, which is linked to the principles of brain gym. One setting I have worked with does a very effective brain gym Zumba with lots of cross-body, bilateral movements and a couple of maracas thrown in for good measure!

How does this intervention session work?

One group of children will be working with an adult having a Dough Gym session. The rest of the children will be split into groups identified by assessment for their need and stage of development. With two adults it is advisable to have no more than five groups in total (including Dough Gym). For example:

Group 1 – Dough Gym
Group 2 – Pom poms and tweezers
Group 3 – Threading on skewers
Group 4 – Spiders in jelly
Group 5 – Zumba.

Firstly, what is Dough Gym?

- Dough Gym is a gym for children where they work out with dough.

- Dough Gym is a specific daily intervention – if it is going to have impact it has to be regular and consistent.

- Dough Gym is exclusive – you need to make the children who need this intervention feel special and chosen for all of the right reasons, not because they are failing. I usually work with a maximum of eight children, not a whole group

- Dough Gym is planned – this initiative is about targeting specific areas of development. It won't work if you just slap a bit of dough around!

- Dough Gym is done to music – I have found that this is key to its success. Children are highly engaged by music and the beat is crucial when it comes to performing the Dough Gym moves. Choose your music carefully. Something that is popular and current is far more likely to get high levels of engagement.

How does a Dough Gym session work?

- Dough Gym needs to take place at the beginning or end of a session so that you are not pulling children out of continuous provision or away from areas of interest and exploration. I always prefer to do mine at the beginning of the day. As you want Dough Gym to carry a bit of prestige and have the 'enviability factor' it is better if it is done in your main space and that children aren't taken off to the Sunshine room to do it! You can run Dough Gym and Funky Fingers (see below) at the same time so that all children are having a daily intervention that is supporting and extending their gross and fine motor development.

Adult role

An adult would need to be stationed with the Dough Gym or other directed activity as children need direct input and will be following constant instruction. The other groups have a task to complete: how many pompoms can you move from the pot to the eggbox with the tweezers? How fast can you fill the skewer with beads and then empty it again? The role of the Dough Gym leader is quite like that of a slightly crazed aerobics instructor. Once the children become familiar with a few basic moves then you will be able to sequence them just by calling out the name of the move when you want the children to change. As the children become more proficient, you add more moves and create a more complex and challenging work-out.

Everyone should know where their Funky Fingers group is and on your command they should take their places! The music goes on and everyone is working at the same time. You will be amazed how tiring working with dough and pompoms can be! The Funky Fingers activities stay for a week. They are only used at Funky Fingers time and not as part of continuous provision. This helps you to ensure that you can really monitor how the children are using them to ensure they have ultimate impact, it also stops the children from getting bored with them.

The easiest way I have found for managing your Funky Fingers time is to have your activities in a box or on a tray under the table in the morning. While one adult is finishing the carpet session another can easily lift the resources out on to the table tops, or you can get the children to do it at the beginning of the session. Once the session is over the boxes go back under the table out of the way. In this session the adult is either leading a specific group or supervising a number of groups.

For further information on how these activities work, see *Getting to Write*; Alistair Bryce Clegg: Featherstone Education; 2013.

5. Virtual base time one

Virtual base times are your adult-directed taught times. They will happen daily and there will be up to three a day depending on the age and ability of your children. In most of the settings I work with, they are usually based around phonics, mathematics and literacy but they could be a taught input about anything.

One of the key things about effective direct teaching in EYFS is that you do it through other areas of learning and development. Actively plan to engage children while getting the maximum coverage of all of the areas of learning.

Why are they called virtual bases?

For me the essence of good Early Years teaching is that it is done through children's interests and promotes high-level engagement. Often this principle gets completely squashed when it comes to carpet-based teaching. The 'base' in 'virtual base' just means a place to gather. It is the 'virtual' bit which is crucial, the 'base' could be anywhere. I called them this to remind practitioners that they shouldn't base their teaching in just one spot (usually the carpet) that they should try and move around their space and teach in different places.

This is good for two main reasons:

1. It helps to maintain levels of engagement for children.

2. It promotes teaching through other areas of learning and development and through other areas of the environment.

If my focus for teaching in mathematics, for example, was counting, rather than get the multi-link and the whiteboards out on the carpet, I would teach counting either using resources that I knew the children would engage with or link the counting to a teaching focus in another area of learning. If it was Autumn then we could get out all of the objects we collected on our Autumn walk, use all of their names, talk about their texture, smell etc. and then count them, thereby teaching a counting focus through Understanding the world. Virtual bases work better the smaller the group of children. Obviously it would be impossible to fit 30 children in your block area or around your workshop table! If you can group your children by their development or ability then this can make your teaching input far more focused.

If your other adults are not comfortable or able to take a group then make sure they are supporting you directly during your teaching of the whole group. Are they sitting near a designated group to give further questioning or support? They should definitely not be carrying out 'housekeeping' duties or sitting on a chair at the side of the carpet while you are teaching.

> ## Adult role
>
> The adult's role is to deliver a planned objective to a designated group of children, often through other areas of the environment and other areas of learning.
>
> This virtual base usually lasts between 10 and 25 minutes depending on the age of the child and their stage of development. If you have got different adults working in different areas of the environment then this allows different groups to have virtual base times of different lengths. If I had a group of children who were at the stage of needing more time to complete an extended piece of writing then I could 'keep' my virtual base group working for a little while longer while the others finished and moved into continuous provision.

6. Continuous provision

The children leave their virtual bases and the adults move with them into continuous provision. At this point the adults would pick up their objective-led planning focus as they will be looking for opportunities to deliver that alongside observing, assessing and generally supporting children's interests. What adults must *not* do is to pick up their objective-led planning and approach it like a tick list, hunting children down! This planning has been put in place to support learning and provide extra focus for attainment, not to dominate learning at all costs.

Children, particularly at earlier ages and stages of development, should always have plenty of opportunities for free, uninterrupted play. Adults should take care that their objective-led planning does not take over.

> ## Adult role
>
> To support children's learning and development both indoors and out using the differentiated provision and objective-led planning. You are probably going to run one more virtual base time before lunch (if it is appropriate for the age and stage of development of your children) so this session of continuous provision should last until then.

7. The brief tidy up

This is not a complete environment overhaul but a brief 're-set' that will allow the following base time to be effective.

8. Virtual base time two

This is your second direct teach of the day (if appropriate). The base time should run under the same principles as before just with a different teaching focus.

Assess and review

At the end of this base time it is a great opportunity to gather together and have a brief assess and review session where the children have the opportunity to talk about what they have done, and adults can make a few 'jottings' as they do.

9. Toilet, hand wash, home/lunch

If you work in a sessional setting you would then repeat the morning programme again for the afternoon group.

In the afternoon (for full time children)

1. Afternoon registration

This can be a quick whip through the register, and then meet on the carpet, when the staff have the opportunity to hear more children read or carry out interventions. This session also provides an opportunity to meet together on the carpet to talk about what the children have done so far today and signpost possible learning opportunities for the afternoon

2. Virtual base time three

This is your third and final direct teach of the day (if appropriate). The base time should run under the same principles as before just with a different teaching focus.

3. Continuous provision

The afternoon session of continuous provision should operate in the same way as the morning's session.

Adult role

To support children's learning and development both indoors and out using the differentiated provision and objective-led planning.

---

4. Tidy-up time

This is your tidy up at the end of the day. Hopefully this slot will get shorter the better children get at tidying up!

5. Carpet session

I like a decent carpet session at the end of the day where you can pull everything

together, swap some stories about how your day has been and then enjoy a good book and a song before the rush to get coats. When you are building in timings to your timetable, try to make some decent provision for both talk and story at the end of the day. Remember that the ideal for emerging readers is to hear at least three stories a day!

Snack, playtime and PE

Three things that don't feature in this timetable are snack, playtime and PE. As I have previously said, you are trying to achieve consistency and flow in children's learning with as few breaks as possible and as a result we need to look carefully at all of the aspects of our practice and provision that cause these learning breaks and then evaluate them for their impact on attainment.

Snack time

When we provide snack for children, what is it for and why are we doing it? There are many aspects of learning and social interaction that can be developed during snack, but usually only if there is an adult there to facilitate them. Snack is a great opportunity to develop language and social interaction, but if children have limited vocabulary and social skills, then they are not going to interact with each other. These skills will not develop on their own.

By the same token you do not want an adult posted at your snack table all day every day. You need a happy medium. You need to treat snack like any other area of continuous provision. It is worth asking the question 'what is snack time for?' before you start to plan for it. At its most basic level, snack is an opportunity for young children, who burn lots of energy in their play and exploration of your environment, to re-fuel. But, in truth there is *so* much more that snack could and should be. At best it can offer some brilliant learning opportunities. At worst it is a bag of apples and some cartons of milk dumped on a table.

Ways of organising snack time

There are a number of ways of running your snack sessions, from 'sit down and eat together' to complete 'free flow'. There should be no hard and fast rule as long as your snack sessions have purpose and are linked to learning as opposed to being a glorified tea party!

At the beginning of your year, or with a new intake of children, you will be stopping and starting your children regularly to re-enforce rules and routines and celebrate individual achievements. During this 'settling in' period, a collective snack time can be brilliant for coaching the children through what snack time is all about. How you eat your snack, how to pour your water and in some cases how to suck through a straw – are trickier than you think if you have never done it before! It is also a time for practitioners to remind children about rules and routines and to celebrate successes.

Another situation where you might consider a 'stop and sit down' snack is to support your key person role. Sharing food is a very social thing to do and meeting and eating in small groups can really help to develop relationships as well as provide fantastic opportunities for adults to tap into children's interests, and then use what they have found out to link into learning for high-level engagement. In one setting the key

adults had a picnic basket complete with blanket, plates and cups. At snack time the children found a space either indoors or out and set up their 'snack picnic'. In this particular setting many of the children lacked a range of vocabulary and talk. So, each week alongside the usual 'chat' we planned in a talk focus. So one week it might have been talk for questioning, another talk for conflict resolution. This didn't mean that this was all that was talked about, but it gave adults a focus for their snack talk, which they could also use in their other interactions with children in and around the setting.

As time goes on and the children get better at using the environment independently, you will do far less stopping and starting as you want to facilitate opportunities for deep level learning, exploration and discovery. This is when a self-service snack comes into it's own. Sometimes practitioners are a bit wary of giving children responsibility for their own snack. Someone did once ask me what I would do if a child took two milks instead of one! I don't think my answer of 'call the milk police and have them arrested' went down too well! There is really no need to be wary though. With some good organisation and high expectations very young children can be very self-sufficient.

Some examples of good practice

> Children at a packaway pre-school self-managing their own snack – including using a toaster without an adult (in a tabard) standing watching. And they do the washing up...

A similar idea is used in some primary schools – for instance, children in a mixed Nursery and Reception group completely self-manage their 'Seedlings café'. The school is in an area of high social deprivation so the café serves breakfast at the beginning of the day. Once the breakfast rush is over, the cereal and toast are replaced with milk, water and fruit. There are two waiters' aprons which the children take turns to wear. They manage the length of time being a waiter by using a timer. The children are surprisingly good at sticking to their time without adult intervention. There are always one or two serial offenders who would keep their apron on all day, but staff are aware of these children and keep an eye out for them. Snack time like this is brilliant for supporting independence and interaction but as there is no adult 'manning' the space it can also become a haven for 'avoiders' who will happy sit and spend half an hour chewing on a piece of apple.

Adult role

Alongside the independence element of the snack area, you also want to introduce other learning opportunities. This can be as simple as having a photograph or an interesting object on the table for the children to look at and talk about. For any continuous provision to be effective, adults need to be mobile within the learning space. You should be taking learning to children rather than pulling children to you. If you set up an activity at a table in one area of your setting and then call children to you it becomes impossible for you to then ensure that what is going on in your continuous provision is really taking children's learning forward and not just low-level holding tasks. So, as an adult moves through the learning space they are able to drop into the snack area, re-set any of the resources that need resetting, check for loiterers and engage in a bit of quality talk. If you are trying to encourage children to talk then you need to give them something that they are going to want to talk about. Humour and terror (within reason) often work well, as does showing them photos of past events, getting them to remember, recall, sequence and articulate their memories. There will also be times when you work in the snack area alongside the children to help them to prepare what they are going to eat and then join them in eating it!

Although I am a fan of keeping most other areas of your provision as ambiguous and open-ended as possible, snack time is one area that you can really go to town on 'dressing'. This not only gives your environment impact but also offers up some great opportunities to reinforce other areas of learning, like role play, mathematics, understanding of the world, mark making – the list is endless! Whether it be a cafe, ice-cream parlour, tea shop, tree house or all-American 1950s diner, just make sure it has purpose and impact as well as good food and quality talk!

Playtime

The EYFS non-statutory guidance talks about 'continuous outdoor access'. The philosophy behind this is that children can not only have access to learning in a completely unique environment, but that they will also be able to continue their learning indoors and out, without breaks. If you have access to an outdoor space then there is no need for your children to stop everything and go out into the playground. Apart from the time that it takes to stop all the activity and get coats on and off, it makes a significant break in children's learning opportunities, interrupts the 'continuousness' of continuous provision and reduces opportunities for objective-led planning.

I usually ask staff to try to compare the progress children make in continuous outdoor provision with the progress they make during playtime. We must keep the one that has the greatest impact on children's learning. With continuous outdoor provision you will be giving children the opportunity to access specific resources for prolonged periods of time where they can develop and enhance their play both individually and with their peers. They have also got time to evaluate and revisit resources as they are part of the provision and not going to be tidied away after 15 minutes. At 'playtime' the children tend to play in a very different way. They will often have a lot of excess energy that they want to get rid of because they have been sedentary indoors. This often results in play that is of a faster pace and more boisterous. There is rarely time for investigation, evaluation and revisiting at playtime, and many school playgrounds are sterile and devoid of the open-ended activities offered within the Early Years classroom or setting.

Timetabled PE lessons

PE is a National Curriculum subject, so there is no legal requirement for children in Early Years to do it as a separate, regular 'lesson'. Having said that, there are lots of unique and enjoyable experiences that you can have in the hall with or without the PE apparatus, that you will not get in exactly the same way in your outside learning area. I think that it is worth having a couple of hall slots booked in on the timetable, but use them as and when you feel it is appropriate to focus on particular physical skills.

The skills of dressing and undressing are important enough to be included in the Early Learning Curriculum, so children do need to practise these at some point, particularly if their parents do everything for them at home, but PE can become a single exercise in the skills of undressing and then dressing again so you need to ensure this doesn't happen. How many times have you turned to see a child who has forgotten where to stop when undressing, and is about to appear stark naked, and how many times have you spent the entire PE session getting socks and shoes off only to have to put them back on again because your allotted time is over? If you wait another half term, the children will be far more dexterous and able to change more quickly, meaning you get more done!

Keys to success

If you get your continuous provision right, then you can be sure that your environment has been created to continue the provision for learning in the absence of an adult. Continuous provision by its very nature means that there may not be an adult in every space guiding children and promoting their learning, and you cannot guarantee that the children who you have aimed specific resources at in specific areas will always go to the area you want them to be in *and* put their hand on the correct resource. What you can say is that through your planning for the provision you have *maximised* the potential for progress and *minimised* the risk of failure.

When you are thinking about your provision can you answer the 'why', 'who', 'how' and 'what' questions?

- Why is it there?
- Who is it there for?
- How will I get the target children to use the provision?
- What skills am I developing?

If you want to get a quick idea of whether your provision is working, then do a few 'on the spot' audits, tracking children who are not working with an adult and trying to equate what they are doing with your intended objectives. But don't beat yourself up when, as you probably will, find that not only are they not honing the right skills, but they are in a totally different area of the room! When children are free to choose what they do, they are open to all sorts of distractions and attractions, and maybe those are much more relevant at the moment than even your carefully prepared beads in jelly!

Another key to the success of your continuous provision is ensuring that the adults in the setting are mobile and constantly moving through the space to support and develop learning. This fluidity cannot happen if all the adults are tied to a space or an activity. If you have created provision linked to assessment that is levelled and dressed for interest then all the adults who are going to work in the space should be aware of what is where and why. When they are moving through the space they will know what they are looking for and will be able to make accurate assessments of whether the provision is being correctly accessed. If it isn't or if a child needs support or challenge, they know which resources to use and how to use them.

Planning

How you plan your day and deliver your teaching is crucial in creating an appropriate environment to allow all of the above to happen. Some of your planning will be done on a daily basis in response to assessments and observations. Some can be done on a weekly basis and tweaked as and when you need to.

Weekly planners

If you were using some of the timetabling, teaching and planning mechanisms that I have talked about in this book, you would need to include them all on your weekly planner, which will have a backbone of the following elements:

- Literacy, mathematics and phonics, or what the focus of each 'virtual base time' is going to be.
- How you will ensure differentiation and indicate which adults will be teaching which groups, and whether this will be on a 'withdrawal' basis (where the children come to the adult) or on an objective-led basis (where the adults go to the children wherever they are).

Virtual or other base time planner

This part of your weekly plan will cover any time when the children will be subject to direct teaching. The 'base' can be the well worn 'carpet' or another place in your setting, indoors or outside. When children are in small groups with an adult, or if you are going to teach your base time objectives through other areas of learning and development, and through other areas of the environment, your weekly plan needs to show which adults will be in which areas of your setting for each base time. This doesn't have to say what they are teaching, just who is going where.

Talk focus for interest carpet times

This just needs to record what type of talk you will be focusing on and any key vocabulary that you would like practitioners to use. This talk will be a predominant focus at carpet (or other base) times, and if adults know what the focus is then they will be able to use it throughout the setting as and when it is appropriate.

Continuous provision during self-registration

If you are going to utilise the beginning of the day to target a specific area of learning in your continuous provision then you would need to record what that was and why you were doing it, referencing assessment data or whole school/setting initiatives.

Funky Fingers/Dough Gym or other targeted activities

Depending on how many groups you have for your five minute physical intervention this could just be a simple activity list indicating any resources needed, with the assumption that the activities will be repeated every day during the week.

Objective-led planner x the number of adults in the room

This is the planning that your adults will be taking with them to support teaching and learning in continuous provision. This planning needs to show which aspect you are going to be teaching. The children's current attainment in the aspect, and their next steps are targets. It is *really* important to remember that this is *not* a tick list and should be delivered across several areas of the environment, and through children's play.

Skill enhancements

If you have identified areas that you feel are stagnating, and you want to enhance them with a skills focus, then your planning should show which areas you are focusing on, differentiation of the skill, and any resourcing that you need to include to support development. If all of this is visible in your setting, it is not only a constant reminder for all practitioners, but it can also help anyone who is coming into your setting to assess progress and learning to know what to look for and also understand how progress works in the Early Years.

Ofsted findings

In Summer 2013, Ofsted produced a report which looked at the ongoing improvement of attainment in some sectors of Foundation Stage provision, and of course, the need for further improvement. The report stated that:

> Since the introduction of the Early Years Foundation Stage the proportion of good or better providers has risen from 64% in 2008 to 74% in 2012, with year-on-year improvements in children's attainment as evidenced by the Early Years Foundation Stage Profile scores. In 2008, 49% of children reached a good level of development; this rose to 64% in 2012. Many providers across all types of early years settings are supporting children's learning well.
>
> However, this masks the fact that two fifths of all early years settings are not improving fast enough to give children the best start in life, including the skills they need to be ready for school. Satisfactory provision is not effective enough to close the attainment gap sufficiently quickly.
>
> Consequently, too few children start school with the knowledge, skills and attitudes they need to make the most of the next stage of their education. Children from poorer families achieve less well than their peers. In 2012, just over a third of children were not working securely in communication, language and literacy, as shown by the Early Years Foundation Stage Profile scores and, in deprived areas, this rose to more than four in 10 children.
>
> (Getting it right first time; Achieving and maintaining high-quality early years provision; Ofsted; 2013)

The report describes features of strong leadership and ways in which leaders, determined to 'get it right first time' for children, have developed and sustained high-quality provision.

> These leaders were clear about which aspects of teaching needed improvement. Commonly, they needed to ensure that staff were:
>
> - prioritising children's communication and language skills, personal, social and emotional development, mathematics and early literacy, and working with parents to help them support their children's development in these areas
> - planning activities based on regular, accurate assessments of children's learning, knowledge and skills, and adjusting activities to meet the needs of individual children and groups who were most at risk of falling behind
> - routinely planning and making the most of structured teaching opportunities each day
> - taking every opportunity when children were initiating their own play to extend children's learning, develop their language, feed in new vocabulary and challenge their thinking
> - developing high-quality questioning skills
> - emphasising the importance of listening carefully to children and thinking about the best time to intervene rather than just jumping in
>
> (Getting it right first time; Achieving and maintaining high-quality early years provision; Ofsted; 2013)

I wholeheartedly agree with all the points above, and would say that they are the aim of most of the practitioners that I work with. The problem is that it is very difficult to facilitate all of the above when you are sitting at a table with a group, counting 'compare bears' on and off a laminated bus! If the report is to affect practice in settings, practitioners must to be in the provision with the children, moving through it. When an adult is working in provision, they are able to challenge, support, observe and teach as well as re-set the environment to ensure that it remains challenging and inspiring and doesn't degenerate into messy pockets of low-level experience. Some 'structured' teaching is an essential part of what we do on a daily basis. It is an opportunity to teach directly, model learning, language and behaviour, and inspire children to make best use of the

environment that we create. Sadly, once children are outside that 'structured' teaching influence, engagement and attainment can drop significantly.

My main issue with grouping children for 'literacy', 'mathematics' and then 'topic', is that the groups are too broad. At this stage of children's development they can excel and need support with different aspects of the same subject area. So I might be a brilliant talker but not such an adept mark maker yet, and despite this, I will be in the same literacy group for both. I might be fantastic at shape but not so great with numbers but I will be in the same mathematics group for both. The answer for me is not to take your children out of continuous provision to 'be taught', but for you to go into play with an objective-led plan.

This chapter contains some examples of planning and time tabling that might help you to evaluate your current planning and decide whether it is a 'best fit' model for you and the children you work with. If there are significant concerns or gaps, inconsistencies or 'hot spots', consider some of the suggestions and whether trying these might make your lives easier and thus more enjoyable.

12 Effective transitions

In an example of good practice, a school and playgroup worked closely together, with nursery recreating the playgroup environment and routines when children first transferred to the school's foundation unit. This close collaboration also ensured that both settings are clear about expectations when children transfer across. There had been a focus on working with other professionals who were involved with the family and ensuring parents were included in the process and were clear about the expectations of the new setting and were aware of the transfer of information about their child.

(Are you ready? Good practice in school readiness; Ofsted; 2012)

The above case study demonstrates clearly that the issues around transition aren't only about the move from Reception to Year One, although the move from the Foundation Stage to Key Stage One has been at the heart of discussions about progress and 'value added' ever since the Foundation Stage Guidance in 2000 advised that:

> *Throughout the family's association with the setting, the key practitioner, parent and child talk regularly to check how well they are all adjusting to the arrangements for settling in, learning and teaching. She makes sure that the family or child's particular interests and experiences, such as the birth of a new baby, are used in planning work with the child. When the child transfers to primary school, the practitioner ensures that the parent knows how to select a school and how the transition will work. She meets the parent to prepare the final record of the child's progress and attainment. She liaises with the receiving school and the family so that everyone is kept fully informed.*

(Curriculum guidance for the foundation stage; QCA; 2000).

Transition or the smoothness of the process of transition is vital if children are not to lose way and experience a dip in both their learning and their sense of wellbeing. In this chapter I have tried to unpick the central issues around transition, *particularly from Reception into Key Stage One*, although the principles for transition are the same whenever it happens. As adults we can find the transitions that we make in our life nerve wracking and unsettling. It could be starting a new job or moving to a new area, and often we don't feel happy and settled until things become a bit more familiar. This sort of feeling is no different for children, in fact it is likely to be greatly magnified. As adults we have a great deal of prior knowledge and experience of life to draw on, children have significantly less. They have probably spent a huge proportion of their waking hours in your setting, and they probably  can't remember a time when *you* weren't there for them.

For many children your setting has provided the stimulation, consistency and stability that they don't have at home. The long working hours of their parents mean they spend time in after school clubs, day nurseries, 'open all hours' care, or child minding before and after their day with you, and even long hours with siblings not much older than them. You are providing a calm and predictable influence in their lives – it's no wonder some children feel totally bereft when they have to move on.

Of course some children move on smoothly, ready for the next challenge, excited about going to 'big school', able to sit still for long periods and ready for the rigour of the National Curriculum. You don't need to worry about these children, they will survive, but in every class or group, there are children for whom this is an event like no other! They don't know from experience that everything is likely to be alright or have strategies for dealing with the situation if it isn't. This is why good transitions are crucial both for children's emotional wellbeing and their potential for attainment.

The greatest inhibitor to both progress and attainment in settings and schools is children's lack of self-confidence and levels of anxiety. When children feel comfortable and 'at home' in their environment they are far more likely to succeed. When they are subjected to significant change it can take many children a long time to adjust to their new situation. During this period of adjustment their potential for maximum progress is drastically reduced. To help to alleviate the anxiety that children might have, it is really useful for approaches to teaching and learning to be harmonised at the point of transition. If children are moving between settings, this can be tricky, but if they are staying with a setting and moving to the next year group it is a far simpler process, although we still should not underestimate the impact of any move from one group to another, even in the most well managed setting.

As well as allowing for some quality time to discuss the transition with all the adults involved, it is really valuable to assess children's emotional welfare, wellbeing and involvement both before and after transition. This will give you an accurate picture of how successful your transition has been. Tools like the Leuven Scales for Wellbeing and

Involvement (see page 13) are a good resource for this. The observations are relatively quick to do, and have been seen to have reliable results.

In many schools and settings, practitioners and their managers feel strongly that children's wellbeing is central to the process of moving from group to group, and school to school. They don't want to rely exclusively on academic attainment scores to measure the success of the process, and use additional information on children's levels of wellbeing and involvement, using the Leuven Scales. It is when children feel most comfortable that there is the most potential to engage them in learning. One thing to keep at the forefront of your thinking is that children should enjoy the transition process, not just experience or endure it, but actually enjoy it, and for this to happen the process needs to be planned well in advance. Practical, pre-transition visits, discussions and activities involving parents are a regular feature throughout the year, not just in the last weeks of the Summer term.

Most importantly, when you are thinking about how to support effective transition it is vital to create a whole setting approach which staff, children, parents, and other agencies clearly understand, and involving everyone in the planning and the process can be very helpful. If children experience a smooth educational and emotional transition from one phase or setting to the next, we know that this will ensure that they make the best all round progress. However, it seems that often they are the last ones that we think to ask! Sometimes the answers children give when we ask them about what it will be like in Year One, are surprising:

Researcher: *What do you think it will be like in Year One?*

Girl: *It is just going to be work, work, work.*

Researcher: *Is there anything you are worried about?*

Girl: *Yes, not being able to play with my friends.*

Boy: *I might not know the words in the books because they have different books and the books in Year One are harder.*

And even after visits:

Researcher: *What do you think it will be like in Year One?*

Girl 1: *I went there for a visit. We will do things like pictures when we go to Year One.*

Girl 2: *I already know because I have been there because we had 'change over classes'.*

Boy: *We went in their class already. Everybody moved up and I went in the Year One class.*

Making a Successful Transition to Year One; NFER Nelson; 2006

Children respond best and settle well when their new environment is very similar to their old one. Obviously you cannot create a carbon copy of the space a child has just left, especially if you are taking your children from more than one setting, but you can have familiar provision and routine. Some schools are able to help by encouraging the allocation of Reception teaching assistants to Year One classes for the first few weeks of the Autumn term, or by adapting the curriculum, or the organisation of the day to be more like the one children are used to.

Transition: The Blackpool Project

It's important that before we start writing policies or changing practice, we think about and agree the principles that underpin our version of transition. Here are some that were agreed by a group of schools during the Blackpool Transition Project (Blackpool Transition Project; Reception to Year 1; 2009/2010):

> The principles that underpin effective transition are:

- Transition is about the setting fitting the child, not the child fitting the setting.
- The transition process is not overlooked or left to chance, but thought about and planned in advance.
- Effective transition takes time, and is a process rather than an event.
- Children should enjoy the transition process.
- The transition should motivate and challenge children.
- Children, parents/carers and staff need to be involved on an equal basis.
- Parents and carers need to feel well informed about and comfortable with all transitions in their child's life.
- There should be agreement on the amount and type of assessment information provided for each child (not too much, not too little).
- There should be a professional regard for the information from the previous setting/ phase.
- Children's emotional welfare, wellbeing and involvement are paramount, and should be assessed before and after transition.
- Approaches to teaching and learning should be harmonised at the point of transition.
- Planning should be based upon assessment information from the previous class/ group/setting.
- Styles of teaching and learning should meet the needs of children and not preconceived notions of what is or is not appropriate for the next phase or stage.
- Staff allocation for a period prior to, during and after initial transition should be adapted to maximise the comfort and welfare of the children.

Although I have included it in the principles, it is worth saying again, transitions are not overlooked or left to chance; good transition takes careful thought and thorough planning well in advance. When adults are as familiar with the children as they can be and the children are as familiar with their new adult and their new space as they can be, then transition will be significantly more effective. Of course, any policy or procedure for transition has to take into account your individual situation and any restrictions or special conditions you may have – these may include:

- the size of your cohort (year group)
- the distance from your setting to the next school
- the number of staff available to support the process
- the funding available to support the release of staff
- the number of children with additional needs (this may restrict the number of extra accompanied visits these children might be able to have)
- the space you have available in your building
- individuals' willingness to be involved (this can be the receiving school, the parents, or even staff in your own school of setting)
- the budget!

In the schools involved in the Blackpool Project, transition from Reception to Year One worked best when the Year One classroom(s) had:

- **areas of continuous provision** to support and extend children's independence skills
- **trained staff** who had received training on how to provide a high quality learning environment
- **staff who had visited Reception** to see how areas of provision provide support and challenge for children's current learning in order to ensure future progress in the way they plan and organise provision in Year One
- **areas of provision in Year One** which were planned for appropriate learning objectives with more challenge and teacher focused tasks
- **access to a richly resourced outdoor classroom to** support teaching and learning in Year One.

Once the children have made the move it can feel like the job is done, but I have found that it makes a significant difference when adults from both sides of the transition process meet after the beginning of the Autumn term, so the new key adult is able to share their perceptions of the children. Of course, the more the adults know about how the process is going to work and what the expectations are, then the more they can help the children. In settings where parents are invited to meetings and other events to explain the process, are encouraged to help in settings and school classrooms, and are given information about the new class or group (for instance the key names of adults, what to do on the first day, what their child might need to bring, and the 'handing over' procedures at the beginning and end of the day) the process is much smoother. Even better, when this information is given before the long summer holiday then parents can support their children and reduce their anxiety.

The most important thing to remember about transition is that effective transition takes time, and is a process rather than an event.

Outcomes of the Blackpool Project (24 children tracked in four schools)

All settings made some progress in improving their procedures, although some was significant and others minimal. All settings were up to date with tracking the wellbeing and involvement of identified children and most had collected both anecdotal and concrete evidence to substantiate their judgements.

The practitioners' personal reflections were available on request, but again these differ significantly in content and reflection. Some were written and some were verbal.

It is this 'difference' that provided a rich breadth of experiences and practice which will then make the finished project accessible to practitioners at all stages of their development.

Alongside the distribution of a 'model' transition policy (see below) to all settings if they wished to use it, I also worked specifically on:

- Systems for providing challenge in continuous provision.
- Staff training to help the staff to reflect on their practice and improve the possibilities for children.
- Asking headteachers to make a definitive statement about their expectations and aspirations for their Early Years and Key Stage One departments and reflect that in the agreed transition policy.
- Providing clear expectations about requirements and time frames for the rest of the project for all participants.

The results of this small piece of research, undertaken in 2009/2010, clearly showed that if transition is to be truly effective in maintaining children's interest and enjoyment in school, which will ultimately impact on their potential for attainment, it must be a carefully considered and valued process. Processes and procedures for transition have improved greatly over the years, particularly since the government and Ofsted have become interested in tracking progress and added value from a child's starting point, not just simple attainment against national standards.

For too many children, especially those living in the most deprived areas, educational failure starts early. Gaps in achievement between the poorest children and their better-off counterparts are clearly established by the age of five. There are strong associations between a child's social background and their readiness for school as measured by their scores on entry into Year 1. Too many children, especially those that are poor, lack a firm grounding in the key skills of communication, language, literacy and mathematics.

(Are you ready? Good practice in school readiness; Ofsted; 2014)

Schools and settings are now very aware that outstanding practice takes the work of everyone, across all the settings and schools attended by the child. If children lose momentum as they move from setting to setting and school to school, the total sum of their progress, and therefore the level of their attainment will be harmed.

Writing and adopting a policy for transition

A Transition Policy is a key document in your transition process, and I have included the skeleton of a policy below (a downloadable copy of the complete policy is available from my blog (www.abcdoes.com/abc-does-a-blog/2010/11/transition-policy).

Once you have constructed and agreed your policy, it will guide your process whenever you are thinking about preparing your children to move on, or up, or over (whatever you call transition in your setting or school).

When you are formulating your policy for transition it is really important that the children and parents are actively involved in the process and their perceptions about transition are explored and valued. In the project work that I have done around transition, I have been able to collect examples of best practice, and construct a Policy Framework that has been used, adapted and adopted by many schools. The initial work was done as part of the project funded by Blackpool Local Authority in 2009/2010. The final report was published and circulated to every Blackpool school, with the sample policy.

Important note

This policy refers to the move from Reception to Year One. The move from class to class, or group to group at younger ages should follow the same process, but should also be easier as the practitioners are, or should already be working closely together.

Transition Policy contents (Reception – KS1)

- Introduction
- Rationale – *why is transition important?*
- Aims – *what do we want to achieve through the process?*

- Equal opportunities and inclusion – *how can we make the process successful for every child?*
- Principles that underpin the policy – *the detail of how the process will happen*
- Initial preparations – *what we need to do first*
- Creating an appropriate environment – *creating an environment for wellbeing*
- Building on what children know and understand – *using assessment to inform the process*
- Partnership with parents – *listening to what parents know, feel, and can do to help*
- Continuing professional development – *issues for the practitioners and teachers*
- Appendices

Introduction

Children grow and develop quickly when they are very young, but with the right support they are more likely to develop specific skills and abilities that will help them succeed in life. Specifically, the early years are a critical time to develop the skills that will prepare them to start school. Early years providers play an important part in this development.

(The report of Her Majesty's Chief Inspector of Education, Children's Services and Skills – Early years; 2014)

Extending the Foundation Stage curriculum into Key Stage One would address the concerns expressed throughout this report, as well as meeting the needs of younger children as they progress through their learning.

In this policy, 'transition' describes the movement that takes place from one year to the next, and in particular from one phase of education to the next within the school. This is different from 'transfer', which usually describes the movement from one school to another.

Rationale

A high quality early years experience provides a firm foundation on which to build future academic, social and emotional success. Key to this is ensuring continuity between all settings, and that children's social, emotional and educational needs are addressed appropriately. Transition should be seen as a process, not an event, and should be planned for and discussed with children and parents. Settings should communicate information, which will secure continuity of experience for the child between settings.

EYFS Practice Guidance; 2009

At [*insert school name*] we feel it is important to create a whole school approach of which staff, children, parents, governors and other agencies have a clear understanding. This policy is a formal statement of intent for Reception to Key Stage One transition. The policy also supports the ways in which we meet the legal requirements of Education Acts and National Curriculum requirements.

Aims

The 'value added' that a school delivers depends on the ability to securely compare pupils' starting points to their end points.

Are you ready? Good practice in school readiness; Ofsted; 2014

We want our children to experience a smooth educational and emotional transition from one phase to the next. This will ensure that children make the best all round progress.

Equal opportunities and inclusion

The children and their parents are actively involved in the process and their perceptions about transition are explored and valued. There are clear curriculum guidelines for children with learning difficulties during transition. Appropriate assistance will be provided in a variety of ways including:

- A range of learning styles.
- Using pupil's ideas and motivations as a starting point for learning.
- Adjusting the conceptual demand of the task as appropriate for the child.

Principles that underpin the policy

The principles that underpin our transition policy are:

- Approaches to teaching and learning should be harmonised at points of transition.
- Planning should be based upon assessment information from the previous class/ group/setting.
- Styles of teaching and learning should meet the needs of children and not preconceived notions of what is, or is not appropriate for the next phase/Key Stage.
- There should be a professional regard for the information from the previous setting/ phase.
- Children's emotional welfare, wellbeing and involvement should be assessed before and after transition.
- Children should enjoy the transition process.
- The transition should motivate and challenge children.
- Staff allocation for a period prior to, during and after initial transition should be made to maximise the comfort and welfare of the children.

- Effective transition takes time, and is a process rather than an event.
- Parents and carers need to feel well informed about and comfortable with all transitions in their child's life.
- Children, parents/carers and staff need to be involved on an equal basis.
- Transition is about the setting fitting the child, not the child fitting the setting.
- Transitions are not overlooked or left to chance, but thought about and planned in advance.

Initial preparations

Transitions are not overlooked or left to chance; good transition takes careful thought and thorough planning well in advance. All staff must be aware of the systems that are currently in place and build this information into the school's Self Evaluation schedule. To ensure that such information is up to date, the following activities take place during the year *before* transition:

- Year One teachers spend some designated time in Reception each term, observing children in their familiar environment and observing practice.
- Reception teachers are given designated time to observe teaching practice in Year One at least once a term.
- Time is planned for termly meetings between Reception and Year One for teachers to discuss ongoing assessment, progress or personal issues connected with individual children, and Profile (EYFSP) information.
- Reception, Year One teachers and the Assessment coordinator meet to agree together what needs to be handed on at the end of the year.
- Reception children visit Year One a minimum of once per term.
- At least one joint project is planned between Reception and Year One to be organised each year. These may take place in Reception or Year One.
- Arrangements are made for passing on information to parents about the transition to Year One.
- Reception parents are invited to meet the Year One teacher/support staff (where practicable) and explore the Year One environment.

Creating an appropriate environment

- Year One classroom(s) have areas of continuous provision to support and extend children's independence skills.
- All staff have received training on how to provide a high quality learning environment.

- Year One staff have visited Reception to see how areas of provision provide support and challenge for children's current learning so that they can ensure future progress in the way they plan and organise their provision.
- The areas of provision in Year One are planned for appropriate learning objectives alongside more challenge and teacher focused tasks.
- Children in Year One have access to an outdoor learning environment to support teaching and learning.
- A richly resourced outdoor area is used to support teaching and learning in Year One.

Building on what children know and understand

- Support staff move temporarily/permanently with Reception children to their next class.
- Reception and Year One staff meet several times during the Summer term to discuss assessment information
- Reception teachers highlight those children who are still working at Foundation Stage level or may need a modified curriculum.
- Year One teachers use cross phase planning that incorporates both Profile Scale Points and National Curriculum levels.
- Teachers meet after the first few weeks in Year One to discuss individual children after the settling in period
- Children return to Reception during the Autumn term to talk about their new classes.
- Throughout the year, Reception and Year One teachers occasionally teach each other's classes to develop a greater understanding of children's learning and gain knowledge about the curriculum.

Partnership with parents

At [school name] we encourage parents and carers to be involved by:

- Inviting them into school three times a year to discuss their child's progress.
- Inviting them into school in the Summer term to discuss their child's annual report.
- Inviting them to curriculum evenings.
- Sending half-termly information booklets/newsletters to inform parents of curriculum coverage.
- Encouraging them to come in and help in the classroom.

Effective transitions

- Giving them information in the Summer term about the class their child will be in.
- Giving clear information about what to expect in Year One.
- Giving them the opportunity to meet the Year One staff before September.
- Inviting them to experience the Year One environment, classroom layout and resources before September.
- Inviting Reception parents to help out in Year One.
- Inviting parents to an information evening outlining what the National Curriculum is, and how best to support their child's learning in Year One.
- Offering brief end of the day 'open door' sessions to parents in the first few weeks of Year One to address any issues regarding their child settling into Year One.
- *[Add examples of your individual practice here]*

Continuing professional development (CPD)

In order to ensure smooth transition from Reception to Year One, the practitioners and teachers at the school meet to discuss and learn abut each others' roles and responsibilities. The result of this CPD is that:

- Reception and Year One teachers know and understand what the Early Years Foundation Stage Profile contains and how to interpret the scale points.
- Reception and Year One teachers know and understand how the Early Years Foundation Stage Curriculum links to the National Curriculum.
- Reception and Year One teachers are confident in making assessments through the observation of children.
- Reception and Year One teachers plan collaboratively checking that both continuity and progression are evident from Reception to Year One.
- Further professional development opportunities in relation to transition are evident in the School Improvement Plan.

Appendices

Could include:

- A resources list
- A transition action plan
- Examples of Profile Point moderation
- References to appropriate relevant information

Further references and reading

- **Seamless Transition**; *Supporting continuity in young people's learning; DFES; 2006*
- **Progress Matters**; *Reviewing and enhancing children's development; DFE; 2009*
- **The report of Her Majesty's Chief Inspector of Education**; *Children's Services and Skills – Early years 2012/13; Ofsted; 2014*
- **Transition in the Early Years**; *Terry Gould; Featherstone Education; 2012*
- **Are you ready? Good practice in school readiness**; *Ofsted; 2012*
- **Getting it right first time**; *Achieving and maintaining high-quality early years provision; 2012*
- **The School inspection handbook**; *Handbook for inspecting schools in England under section 5 of the Education Act 2005; Ofsted; 2015*

When you have read this chapter, you will understand that the process of moving on/up/over provides children and the adults who work with them with anxieties, challenges and questions! However, given time and collaboration, most of these can be alleviated, to provide truly smooth transitions.

And finally...

This book has covered a wide number of issues of current concern to Early Years practitioners. From the first chapter covering the Characteristics of Effective Learning, to the last, where I reflect on the issues around transition, this rather idiosyncratic wander through the implications of working with the EYFS, is intended to help you reflect on your own practice at a time when the Ofsted goalposts are moving once again.

I hope that I have emphasised the importance of wellbeing enough to enthuse you to raise its profile in your setting, and helped you to review the organisation and management of learning, so you can balance child initiated learning, continuous provision, and adult-led activities in a way that doesn't impact on children's freedom to learn though play. I've considered ways to maintain the thrill of learning while planning the practice of basic skills, and along with everything else, I hope I have helped you to make sense of all that time you spend observing the children, making it purposeful for learning, but also enabling you to demonstrate progress and attainment across your whole group, using the same information to celebrate achievement, while planning for the future.

Teaching is all about capturing the moment for individuals, and not wasting a moment of their time in the Early Years. Remember what two boys said about carpet time in Year One:

Researcher: Is there anything you don't like about being in year 1?

First Boy: Being on the carpet for a long time.

Second Boy: Neither do I because it's very boring.

First Boy: And it wastes our playing time.

Second Boy: It wastes your life.

(Making a Successful Transition to Year One; NFER Nelson; 2006)